D0185907

MANCHESTER AT WAR

Compiled and written
by Clive Hardy

First Edition Limited

The first edition of this book was written by the author and published by Archive Publications Ltd in 1986

First published in 2005 by: First Edition Limited,
32 Stamford Street, Altrincham, Cheshire, WA14 1EY
in conjunction with MEN Syndication, 164 Deansgate,
Manchester, M3 3RN.

ISBN: 1-84547-096-6

Introduction to the Second Edition

Welcome to the second edition of Manchester at War and those of you familiar with the first edition will see that there is very little similarity between the two. First and foremost this is not a blow by blow account of the war years, neither is it an academic work. What I hope it is, is an illustrated in-sight into the people, places and events of one of the most fascinating periods of our recent history.

This edition opens with a look at life during the Hungry Thirties when life for the average northern working class person could be a battle for survival. At the same time affluent middle-class homeowners in the south east were buying household appliances, running motorcars, and developing a taste for holidays abroad.

The section on the Home Front takes a look at rationing, make-do-and-mend, the black market, entertainment, work and leisure as well as air raid precautions and civil defence. There is of course a major section covering the Christmas Blitz of December 1940 and a number of pictures from several raids in 1941 are also included. What I have done with some of these captions is to give both the original as written by either the Manchester Guardian or Evening News copy writer, and the one subsequently used after the picture had been submitted to the Press & Censorship Bureau.

Hitting Back takes a look at the armed forces and merchant navy. There are pictures of the 8th (Ardwick) Battalion, Manchester Regiment, Home Guard units on parade and at a street fighting school, and the ATS.

Just a word about prices, which are given in pounds, shillings and pence – a straight decimal conversion is meaningless. For example 27/3d converts to £1.36p but to get some idea of its buying power in 1936 we need to multiply it by 40, making it £54.40p. Measurements are given in miles, yards, feet and inches: weights are in imperial units, and the pumping capacities of fire appliances etc are given in gallons. So you can have lots of fun converting them to new money should you feel the need.

Above all this book is about dibbing in and out. Welcome to what is and what was Manchester at War.

Clive Hardy.
October 2005

THE HUNGRY THIRTIES

In October 1929, a brand new luxury apartment on New York's plush Fifth Avenue cost around $6000 a week to rent and tickets to one of the hit Broadway shows averaged out at $28 each. By the end of the following month, the Fifth Avenue apartment could be rented for less than $500 a week and theatre tickets were down to two or three dollars apiece. The financial crisis caused by the collapse of the New York Stock Exchange had begun to bite.

American industry had grown fast and fat since the end of the First World War, due to a deliberate policy of readily available loans from the Federal Reserve Bank. At the same time ordinary American s were encouraged to speculate with stock even to the extent of taking out loans to make purchases. As the paper value stock spiralled ever upwards, the more people borrowed to buy more stock, the more they spent on cars, apartments, household appliances and generally having a good time. By the time private car ownership in Britain stood at 1,157,344 it had already passed the 23million mark in the USA. At the same time the US was lending money to Europe on an unprecedented scale. Between 1925 and 1929 it amounted to no less than $2,900million.

In July 1929 the America's very own South Sea Bubble finally burst as the big boys, sensing it was time to get out, took their money and ran for cover. Stock prices tumbled, banks called in loans, and stock prices fell even further. By the end of October $18,000million had been wiped off the value of US companies but this was just the beginning. Despite a price rally during the early months of 1930 confidence again slipped and by June the market was on a downward slide that would last unabated for twenty-five months. By mid 1930 the effect of the Wall Street Crash was severe; trade was declining, markets shrinking and prices falling. There was a sharp rise in unemployment in the UK, due to the downturn in export orders to the US. Those who qualified for dole money lived in dread of a visit from the public assistance man who could turn up on the doorstep at any time of the day or night. All who applied for Means Tested benefits were subjected to questioning of a personal nature that was often searching, often impertinent, but failure to answer would result in dole money being cut or withdrawn altogether. And, just to compound the problem Australia suddenly imposed a ban on immigration which was to last until the industrial slump had abated. In an effort to provide employment in the hardest hit areas J H Thomas, Lord Privy Seal, brought in a series of road and rail improvement schemes. These schemes provided much needed work but much of it was short-term stuff. In Cornwall out-of-work tin miners found employment for a few months widening the roads between Penzance and Hayle, and Penzance and Torpoint. Manchester also embarked on a major programme of road improvements, the biggest projects being the reconstruction of

The first stage of Manchester's new bus station in Piccadilly takes shape during 1931. In the background the Ryland's building (later Paulden's) is nearing completion. Designed by Ted Adams, the Ryland's building was primarily a warehouse with provision for retail outlets on the ground and first floors. The Market Street facade was 230ft long: Marks & Spencer took up most of the corner on High Street and Dolcis Shoes were on the Tib Street corner.

the roads to Altrincham and Sale. The early thirties also saw Manchester embark on a major housing project when work began on building the Wythenshawe estate. It was estimated that at least 89,000 people were living two or more to a room in Liverpool. In Birmingham the figure was put at 68,000 and for Manchester it was 49,000. Sir Ernest Simon described the conditions he found in one house in the slum district of Angel Meadow. 'The general appearance and condition of this house is very miserable. It is dark and the plaster on the passage walls, in particular, was in a bad condition. There is no sink or tap in the house; they are in a small yard, consequently in frosty weather the family is without water. In the house live a man and wife, seven children, ranging in age from fifteen to one, and a very large, if varying, number of rats.' Sir Ernest planned to house 100,000 people on the 2,500 acre Wythenshawe estate and by 1939 seven thousand houses had been built and plans had also been drawn up for a large-scale redevelopment of the southern half of the city. There were drawbacks for people living at Wythenshawe. They had to have their own transport or rely on corporation buses, not only to get to work, but also for shopping, entertainment and leisure, as the estate lacked shops and pubs and there was no cinema. It would be the 1960s before Wythenshawe got its own shopping centre.

For several years Britain had already been feeling the effects of overseas competition and traditional industries such as mining, shipbuilding and iron and steel making were bearing the brunt, but Lancashire cotton was also starting to suffer. Since the late 1920s the Indian Congress Party had been demanding independence and in 1930 Mahatma Gandhi had been advocating a boycott of British goods, especially cotton. But while Britain was already declining and had two million on the dole, several European countries including Czechoslovakia, Austria, and Germany were enjoying a period of relative prosperity with full order books and growing exports. However it didn't last for much longer as US investors withdrew funds to service ever mounting debts at home.

Early in 1931 the Kredit Anstalt bank of Austria finally went bust: the country being kept afloat by a guarantee from the Bank of International Settlement and a loan from the Bank of England. Speculators began to twitch and pull their money out of Central Europe. Worse was to come as German banks began to fail. Germany was groaning under reparations payments to the French who refused point blank to ease off. During the summer severe financial strain was placed on London as foreigners turned their holdings into gold, forcing the Bank of England in turn to borrow gold from France and the USA. On 21 September the government abandoned the gold standard: the immediate effect being the devaluation of the pound from $4.86 to $3.49. The Labour government, already struggling against the slump and a rising dole queue, was unable to get to grips with the economy. In desperation the Ramsey MacDonald went to the palace to resign, returning to announce that along with a handful of Labour MPs the Conservatives and the Liberals he would form a national government. At the ensuing general election National government candidates took 554 seats against 52 Labour.

Between 1931 and 1935, Government economic cuts resulted in dole rates being set at survival level. For example a man with a wife and three children to support received just 29/3d a week in either benefit or 'transitional payments' once his entitlement to benefit had been exhausted. Transitional payments were subject to the means testing, a particularly vicious piece of legislation under which the earnings, savings, pensions and other assets of a family were taken into account before an award was made. It was automatically assumed that the assets of the family were available to support the unemployed man. Children if in work - even a paper round counted - and if they lived at home, were expected to support out of work parents. If a family received a gift - such as a food parcel from a relative - it had to be declared and the value of the parcel's contents was then deducted from the next payment. Neighbours were positively encouraged to spy and inform on one another. Large numbers were cut off from benefit by the Means Test. It has been claimed that in Lancashire over a third of all applicants were refused help. The unemployed felt that the Means Test was class-betrayal by Ramsey MacDonald and other senior Labour figures who were now despised as traitors.

One of Labour's more able members, Sir Oswald Moseley, Chancellor of the Duchy of Lancaster, had already left the government because the Cabinet had failed to agree to his scheme for bringing down unemployment. Moseley's suggestions included more money being committed to public works programmes, the school leaving age being raised by one year, the introduction of early retirement on a liveable pension, and the control of credit through the banks. Moseley and his followers formed the New Party that eventually became the British Union of Fascists (BUF).

Up to abandonment of the gold standard Britain had weathered the US slump reasonably well as trade with the Empire, apart from India, hadn't been affected too much, but the devaluation was a further blow to those shipping companies operating UK-USA services. By the spring of 1932 more than 30per cent of British registered ships were laid up, leaving thousands of merchant seaman jobless. But as they say 'one man's meat is another man's poison' and Truro Corporation was raking in the money from fees charged on over 143,000 tons of merchant shipping laid up in waters under its control. It was a similar story in Scotland where those local authorities with jurisdiction over certain sea locks were offering lay-up facilities at competitive rates.

Manchester Liners were hit by the downturn and were forced to lay up several ships. Of these the Manchester Merchant was eventually sold for breaking up and Manchester Civilian was sold to Greek owners. When the 1933 'summer' season of sailings to Quebec and Montreal commenced, the company ran the service with just six vessels Manchester Regiment, Manchester Brigade, Manchester Commerce, Manchester Citizen, Manchester Division and Manchester Producer. As the economic situation improved the company ordered new tonnage from Blytheswood Shipbuilding on the Clyde and the fast cargo liner Manchester Port was delivered during 1935. She was followed in 1937 by the Manchester City and in 1938 by Manchester Progress. The new ships enabled Liners to dispose of Manchester Hero and Manchester Producer.

The ghostly blur of a motorcyclist flashes past a policeman on point duty on Walmsley's corner of the Victoria Buildings. Chain stores - those with twenty-five or more branches, increased from 20,602 in 1920 to 39,013 by 1939. Bigger chains - those with over 200 branches, increased during the same period from 10,942 to 21,283. During the inter-war period, the Co-op accounted for ten per cent of all high street business.

Britain cancelled Germany's reparation payments in 1932. The British Government then applied to the USA for the cancellation of our debt to them. Unfortunately America was feeling the pinch and refused. France, though raking in money from Germany, simply defaulted on her debt repayments to the USA. Inspired by this show of Gallic indifference, Britain followed suit, making only one more repayment: and a token one at that before forgetting altogether.

On 23 August 1931, the Labour Government collapsed to be replaced by a coalition National Government that included members of the three main political parties. The move wasn't unopposed.The bulk of the Parliamentary Labour Party believed its leaders had been railroaded into betraying the party's fundamental socialist principles. On 9 September, the new government brought in an Economy Bill; in effect an immediate ten per cent cut across the board in Government spending, including unemployment benefits. The National Unemployed Workers Movement organised a National Hunger March from the worst affected provinces to London, where they would hand over a petition signed by more than one million people calling for the abolition of the Means Test and the restoration of the ten per cent cuts. The bulky petition was deposited for safe keeping at an underground railway station cloakroom while the NUWM held a rally on Hyde Park, but when they went back to collect it, it had been 'lost.' Our picture shows the Scottish and Lancashire contingents passing through Manchester.

The Special Areas Act of 1934 set aside £2million to assist workers from areas worst affected by the depression in relocating to more prosperous parts of the country. The fund also provided incentives to companies to open factories in the deprived areas. There were jobs to be had in the south east even if they were mainly white collar, though that in itself was one of the factors that was feeding a building boom around Greater London. The burgeoning middle-class could spend its money on a telephone – there were two million private phones by 1934 – or on a Hoover (cost £10.15s), or perhaps on one a washing machine (£40). Whilst the south east was weathering the storm reasonably well, unemployment in Jarrow had reached 67.8 per cent, 44.23 per cent in Gateshead, and 61.9 per cent in Merthyr. Of the thirty-three pits that were active in the Bishop Auckland area of County Durham in the late 1920s only thirteen were now winding coal, and of the 28,000 miners once employed there, only 6,500 were left and most of them were working part-time.
During the depression output from Manchester area collieries was regulated under the Lancashire and Cheshire (Coal Mine) Scheme of 1931. Manchester Collieries formed in March 1929, an amalgamation of a number of companies: Astley & Tyldesley Collieries; Clifton & Kersley Coal Co; Fletcher, Burrows & Co; Andrew Knowles & Sons, and John Speakman & Sons. Bridgewater Collieries and Bridgewater Wharves retained their separate identity until 1934 though they too

On 1 October 1931, several hundred demonstrators organised by the NUWM gathered in the square in front of Salford Town Hall to protest at the cut in unemployment benefit. A pitched battle with police broke out and twelve demonstrators were arrested. A week later 5,000 gathered at Ardwick Green, their intention being to march in an orderly manner to Manchester Town Hall where they would hand in a petition. When the police informed the March organisers that their intended route was considered 'provocative' fighting once again broke out. The following day Manchester witnessed scenes reminiscent of the General Strike with police mounting guard on public buildings and the mobilisation of special constables on an unprecedented scale.

were part of the organisation. Developments included the construction of new screens at Mosley Common No4 Pit, new headgear and a reconstructed washery at Sandhole No2 Pit, and a new washery at Astley Green. The company actively pursued the acquisition of collieries that were on the point of closure – such as the West Leigh Colliery Co – not to save them but to get their hands on the coal quota. Another was Shakerley Colliery Co, which had remained outside the 1929 merger, though in 1935 its directors finally agreed to sell. Output from Shakerley's Wellington Pit was quickly run down and it was abandoned in May 1935, with the Nelson Pit following in October 1938. Other closures included Clifton Hall Colliery near Pendlebury, which closed soon after the amalgamation, though nearby Wheatsheaf Colliery was reconstructed. Pendleton Colliery was given a new steel headgear during 1931 even though output was falling. By April 1939 the Rams seam was exhausted and the colliery finally closed. During the war the Manchester Oxide Co opened a plant for reprocessing spent iron oxide on the site of Pendleton Colliery screens.

By the beginning of 1935 rearmament was taking up industrial slack as lead items for battleships, aircraft carriers and cruisers were ordered, and design contracts for new aircraft, armoured vehicles and artillery placed. Within two years the rearmament programme had seen some expansion within coal mining, shipbuilding and iron and steel making. Employment received a further boost with the Special Areas (Amendment) Act which incorporated proposals by Sir Malcolm Stewart that in return for opening a factory in a depressed area, a company should be awarded tax, rent and rates incentives for a period of not less than five years. Sir Malcolm's ideas led directly to the creation of a number of trading estates where companies could move into ready-built facilities. Initially these estates attracted only light industries but by the end of the year unemployment in the Special Areas had fallen by a healthy 155,000 although 67,000 of these people had in fact moved elsewhere in search of work. By 1939 over 500,000 workers were employed in light industries such as plastics or the manufacture of telephones and military and household equipment in Bakelite.

It is November 1931 and several small boys help the cook at Chetham's Hospital to mix the Christmas puddings.

A hundred – maybe even two hundred years ago, this scene from 1938 would have been familiar to anyone visiting the heart of Manchester. Spring sunshine lights up young faces in the ancient doorway of Chetham's Hospital.

At dinner time unemployed men could, for a few pence, buy a hot meal at the Society of Friends' meeting house on Mount Street.

Some of Salford's unemployed men whiled away part of their time by attempting to keep fit. This picture was taken at Great Clowes Street Drill Hall.

A sign of the times is this queue on interview day at the Queen's Park Hippodrome. With thirty jobs on offer, the queue had started forming at 5.30am and by the time the Manchester Guardian photographer turned up more than a thousand people had lined up.

The scene is Whitworth Street in 1930 and cars had yet to become a familiar sight on Manchester's roads, but police were already making checks. The two policemen have their backs to the old fire station which came to symbolise the city's defiance in the face of the German onslaught during the war.

By 1931 Britain's commercial locomotive manufacturing industry, which included Beyer Peacock & Co, Gorton and the Vulcan Foundry at Newton-le-Willows, was suffering from a down-turn in orders for new engines. That year Nasmyth Wilson & Co completed just two engines - their lowest output since 1893. Our picture was taken in 1936; the firm's best year since 1930, with eighteen engines being completed, including this one for China. The following year twelve engines were built, and in 1938 it was down even further to just four. Nasmyth Wilson was wound up in 1939.

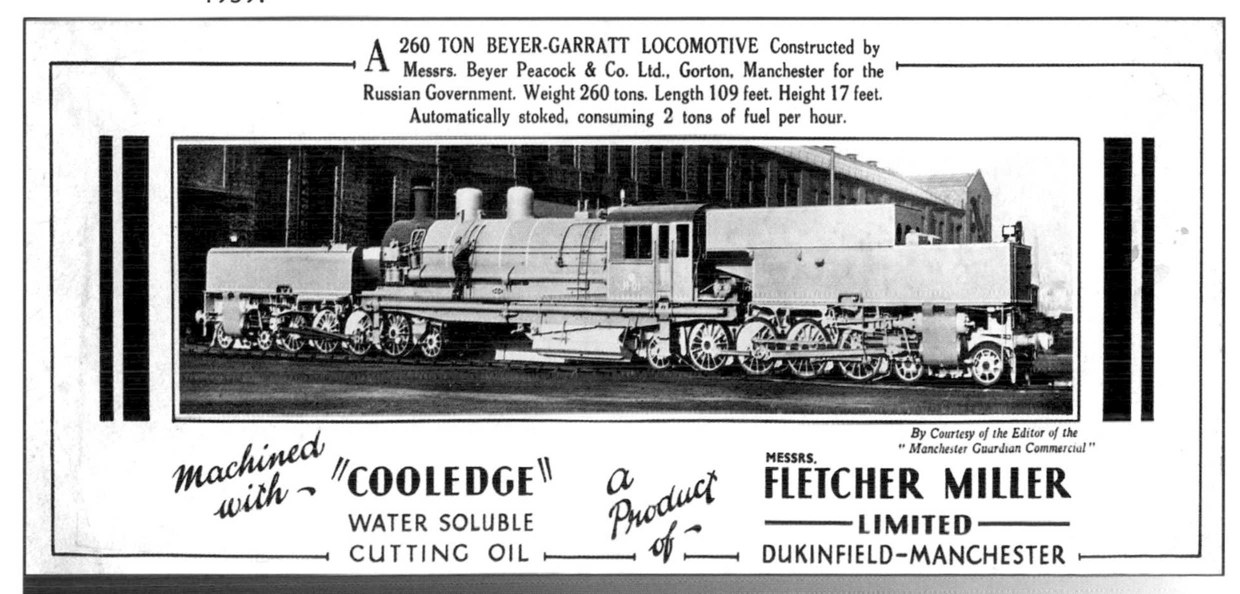

During the thirties locomotive manufacturer Beyer Peacock & Co almost went bust as new orders dried up. Orders dropped from ninety-six in 1930 to just twelve in 1932. The biggest locomotive built by the firm during the thirties was this monster for the USSR.

When this picture was taken in Salford in February 1933, the area was already scheduled for demolition under a slum clearance programme.

A Salvation Army mobile canteen doles out tea, coffee and sandwiches to unemployed men on 30 December 1931.

First published in the Evening News on 20 April 1936, this picture shows the conditions faced by commuters during the morning rush-to-work. 'Tramcars and motor traffic had to use lamps, and there were general doubts about the accuracy of the calendar which assured us this was the second day of summer-time.'

Manchester Corporation had a cunning plan to beat the thick fog that played havoc with its motorbus services. Meet the fog pilot, a motorcycle combination equipped with powerful lamps front and back. The idea was simple. During thick fog the bike would take the lead and the bus would hopefully follow. The idea was also sound providing the motorcyclist didn't lose his way either.

All Saints towards the end of March 1937. Note the shop on the extreme right of the picture is already decorated for the forthcoming Coronation of King George VI.

The sight and sounds of cotton mill girls were once a part of everyday life. So much so that Alderman M B Farr (Socialist) of Mossley, suggested that the council should give one of its allocation of tickets to the Coronation to a local mill girl so that she could represent Mossley's cotton workers. Only one other member of the Council, Councillor Martin, supported Alderman Farr: the Mayor (Alderman Laming) ruling that Councillors must have first refusal. The tickets went to Councillor Rawson who had decided to take his daughter.

Manchester's streets were decked-out for the Coronation. The Coronation of King George and Queen Elizabeth was, at the time, the most expensive ever staged, costing London £524,000: enough money to provide the RAF with at least ten squadrons of the new Spitfire Mk IA then under development. A further £218,000 was allocated from the Defence Budget to cover the cost of troops present. The Coronation of King George V in 1911 had cost the capital £185,000, while that of King Edward VII in 1902 had been a slightly more expensive bun fight at £193,000. Needless to say local authority expenditure spent on celebrating the Coronation came in for strong criticism from the unemployed, who believed the money could have been better spent.

Sunlight and shadow at Cromford House, Cromford Court, off Market Street in 1938.

This picture is thought to be of the queue for jobs at the Paramount cinema.

Retained for a second week at the Paramount Theatre in September 1931 was the six-reel comedy *The Devil To Pay* starring Ronald Colman and Lorette Young (seen here) ably supported by Myrna Loy and Frederick Kerr. The film was described by the *New York Herald Tribune* as being '..a polished, tasteful and entirely likeable screen comedy.'

Binnie Barns, the British actress who played the role of 1880s American stage star Lillian Russell in Universal Picture's *Diamond Jim*, a comedy drama written by Preston Sturges and directed by A Edward Sutherland. Sturges, who developed a reputation for penning off-the-wall comedies went on to become a successful director in his own right. His wartime output included the 1940 releases *Christmas in July* and *The Great McGinty*. In 1941 he directed *Sullivan's Travels* and *The Lady Eve*, and these were followed in 1942 with *The Palm Beach Story* and *The Miracle of Morgan's Creek* in 1943. In 1944 he directed *Hail The Conquering Hero* and *The Great Moment*.

An unlikely pairing by 20th Century Fox was that of Irish-American Brian Donlevy and Rochdale lass Gracie Fields in the 1938 movie *We're Going to Be Rich*. It was Donlevy's fourth picture and Fields' ninth. Set in the South African goldfields of the 1880s, it tells the story of a singer who leaves her no-good husband for a guy who runs a pub.

THE LIGHTS GO OUT

Hitler was without doubt a charismatic figure, adept at political rhetoric he reached into the consciousness of a people who had been humiliated by the Treaty of Versailles and mass unemployment problems. Hitler offered a demoralised nation the chance of prosperity and restoration of national pride – and, whether we like it or no, he delivered it. Political opportunist he may well have been, but he was also totally committed in his desire to see Germany once more established as the leading European power.

On 9 March 1935 Germany formally acknowledged that she possessed an air force (Luftwaffe) and a week later conscription was introduced to raise the strength of the army from 100,000 to 550,000 men. During 1936 Hitler ordered his reinforced army into the demilitarised Rhineland, and when Britain and France failed to do anything about it the Fuhrer instinctively knew that the diplomatic initiative in future European affairs lay with himself. On 5 November 1937, the Fuhrer met in secret with his military advisers and told them of his desire to see an enlarged Reich through unification with Austria (Anschluss) and the annexation of those parts of Czechoslovakia where the majority of the population were ethnic Germans. Any further territorial expansion would have to be accomplished by 1943, or at the latest by 1945, as it was estimated that Germany's military advantage would be worn away by then as other powers rearmed.

German troops crossed the Austrian border unopposed on 11 March 1938 and the following day Austria was annexed. Within forty-eight hours of the invasion Hitler was riding in triumph through the streets of Vienna.

Towards the end of April 1938 Britain and France appeared at last to be waking up to what Germany was up to, as the first in a series of meetings were held to discuss the implications of German intentions towards the Czechs. On 4 September the Czech Government finally cracked. Fearing civil war and unable or unwilling to act without French, British, or Russian support, President Benes agreed to certain Sudeten demands.

Neville Chamberlain flew to Bechtesgaden. During their three-hour meeting Hitler made it quite plain that unless Britain accepted Germany's claims there was little point in talking. Chamberlain, in no position to negotiate an on-the-spot agreement offered to consult with his Cabinet if in the meantime Germany refrained from opening hostilities. Hitler agreed.

As the situation deteriorated, air-raid trenches were hurriedly dug in public parks the length and breadth of Britain – even in towns far beyond the range of the Luftwaffe bombers – and our inadequate anti-aircraft batteries trundled into position around London and one or two other select places. Around 38million gasmasks were distributed to the civilian population, many of them put together by schoolchildren taught to assemble them in their classrooms. The process of stretching the thick rubber bands over the filters left many children with raw thumbs for weeks afterwards. Stocks of emergency coffins were also prepared but as far as is known the children weren't involved with these.

Hitler having squandered the chance to launch a pre-emptive strike agreed to meet with Chamberlain at Munich. By the time Chamberlain flew out on the 29th, some sections of the British population were already panic buying food, petrol and fuel. Those with the means headed out of London for quieter climes where the chances of the Luftwaffe dropping the odd bomb or two were considered remote. Gas masks were issued to all civilians except babies – there weren't any for the youngest members of the population, and the major railway companies were asked to schedule special evacuation trains should the need arise to evacuate women and children from the capital.

Munich opened without Czechoslovakia or the Soviet Union being represented. Despite the French sabre rattling the conference was little more than a sham. Chamberlain was determined to cling to his policy of appeasement. Chamberlain and Hitler, on the initiative of the former, signed a declaration that the two countries would in future settle any differences by negotiation.

Hitler's hunger for power ensured that this agreement was worthless. At 4.40am on 1 September, the German battleship *Schleswig-Holstein* conveniently moored in the port of Danzig (Gdansk) on a friendship visit opened fire at close-range on the Polish fortifications at Westerplatte. Within the hour German armoured units had crossed into Polish territory and the Luftwaffe had launched raids upon Warsaw, Lodz, Czestochowa, Cracow and Poznan.

In England the War Office issued instructions to the Regular Army and all Territorial units that general mobilisation had been proclaimed and that all troops should report to their depots. Under the Defence Regulations, the blackout came into effect at sunset and would last for 2,061 consecutive nights.

At 7.30pm Neville Chamberlain rose in the Commons. Members of both sides had expected to be told that an ultimatum had been delivered to Berlin. Instead they were treated to the news that there was still the possibility of a conference if Hitler withdrew his troops. Chamberlain sat down. There were no cheers, no applause – just silence. The acting Labour leader Arthur Greenwood rose to his feet and encouraged by members of all parties spoke: 'Every minute's delay now means loss of life, imperilling our national interests …I wonder how long we are prepared to vacillate.' That night Cabinet members Hore-Belisha, Anderson, Colville, de la Warr, Dorman-Smith, Stanley, Wallace, and Elliot met with Sir John Simon. Later Simon went to the PM and told him bluntly that the Cabinet would no longer co-operate with him unless war was declared. At last Chamberlain spoke. 'Right, gentlemen, this means war.' Almost simultaneously a tremendous clap of thunder rolled over London as a storm of Old Testament proportions set in.

At 9.00am on Sunday 3 September 1939, an ultimatum was delivered to Berlin. It expired two hours later without reply. At 11.15am Chamberlain broadcast his now famous speech on the radio. We were at war.

The outbreak of war didn't catch Britain with its trousers down. Throughout the year various organisations had been preparing for what many regarded as inevitable. During July no less than 34,000 militiamen had been called up for training. Even then *The Times'*, City Editor, Norman Crump, was still getting it wrong, writing that 'war was unlikely,' as Germany was impressed by Britain's rapid rearmament. That same month women aged 17 to 62 were invited to attend interviews for the proposed Land Army and a number of towns were reporting that the recruiting of men aged between 30 and 50 for the Special Constabulary was going well. The British Medical Association discussed problems associated with the long-term storage of food and the manufacture and storage of vitamin supplements and wholesale meat suppliers were registering under a scheme for the control of meat and livestock should war come. Plans were also being drawn up to ensure that road traffic could continue moving during blackouts. Among the measures was the painting of distinguishing lines on trees, curbs, lamp posts and so on.

Neville Chamberlain inspects a guard of honour before boarding a plane at Cologne airport to bring him back to England. Already nearly seventy years old, the hawkish-looking Chamberlain had been Minister of Health in the Conservative Government of 1924-1929 and more recently Chancellor of the Exchequer in the National Government. As Prime Minister however he would prove obstinate, secretive, arrogant, and impatient of criticism. He ruled his Cabinet with a rod of iron and would, if necessary, ignore Parliament, avoid debate, and circumvent officials. Chamberlain embarked on what he himself called a 'general scheme of appeasement' as the way to solve all of Europe's problems and save us from ever again facing the ravages, horror, and slaughter of World War One. But by 1937 Europe was already heading inexorably towards a far bloodier conflict in which man's inhumanity to man would sink to new depths.

Early in 1939 it was announced that there was to be a doubling of the strength of the Territorial Army. Taken on 19 April, our picture shows recruits to the 65th (Manchester) AA Regiment RA attending a drill night. They might not have uniforms but at least they do have a gun - even if it is a veteran of the Great War.

It is the 1 April 1939 and the territorial battalions of the Manchester Regiment are having a recruiting drive. Here final adjustments are made to a Bren gun mounted on an anti-aircraft tripod as the 9th Manchesters prepare to tour the city.

From the end of July 1939 tribunals were being heard for those people objecting to service under the Military Training Act on pacifist, religious or political grounds. Altogether 59,000 claimed objection and of these 14,500 volunteered for non-combatant roles within the armed forces, 28,500 were allowed to register provided they stayed in their current jobs or agreed to undertake approved work. About 3,500 people were given unconditional exemption and over 12,000 were turned down flat. Some of our bravest bomb disposal, fire service, and ARP rescue personnel were conscientious objectors and many of them gave their lives doing their duty.

4th SEPTEMBER, 1939

GOLD MUST BE SOLD TO THE TREASURY

BILLETS BY ORDER, IF—

Cinemas, Theatres Close to Cut Risks

HITLER BLAMES BRITAIN

PETROL IS RATIONED

BANKS ARE SHUT TO-DAY

Armour's Veribest Corned Beef Grade "A"

AIR MAIL CURTAILED

U.S. REFUGEES LEAVE LONDON

DUKE TAKES UP NAVAL POST

Day-old Babies Leave

WARNINGS TO SHIPPING

Waiting to register at a local recruiting office.

IMPORTANT

NATIONAL EMERGENCY

IMPORTANT

BE PREPARED

EVERY PERSON—YOUNG OR OLD—
SHOULD WEAR OUR

Identity Discs

Full Name and Address—Plainly and Permanently Engraved
on Aluminium—Non-Rusting—Can Be Worn Next the Body

Ensure You and Your Family Carry On Their Person Correct
Identity Details—*ESPECIALLY THE CHILDREN*

IDENTITY DISCS FOR CHILDREN—WHERE DESIRED
THE EVACUATION GROUP NUMBER WILL BE SHOWN

Manufactured to be worn suspended round the neck—easily concealed

PRICE **1/-** EACH DISC

ONLY OBTAINABLE FROM
"Identity Disc," LEEDS PLACE, TOLLINGTON PARK, LONDON, N.4.

TO ORDER:—Forward P.O. value 1/- for EACH Disc, made
out to "Identity Disc" and crossed /& Co./, also enclose
a stamped (1½d.) addressed envelope and full details.

IMMEDIATE DELIVERY. LAST A LIFETIME.

Though Barton Bus Company's main depot was at Long Eaton on the Nottinghamshire/Derbyshire border they operated road tours all over Britain. This picture was taken in late August 1939 during their first Continental Road Cruise – the first ever to be organised by a British bus company. Lasting twelve days, the tour started from Dover and took in Belgium, Germany and France, and cost twenty-three guineas per person, including first class rail travel to the port from London, full accommodation throughout the tour and all gratuities. The bus was packed and included four people from Manchester, two from Altrincham, and three from St Annes. And this was in the days before roll-on roll-off, so the bus had to be craned on and off the ferries. The tour got back to England on 28 August.

Evacuation

As the international situation deteriorated throughout the summer of 1939, local authorities in those towns and cities thought to be most at risk from bombing urged parents to come forward and register their children for evacuation to designated safe areas and by mid-July some authorities were already holding evacuation rehearsals. Yet despite a wealth of publicity the number of children registered fell far short of government expectations and when the evacuations got under way in earnest the numbers that actually went would vary dramatically from one place to another. On the morning of 31 August, education committees across the nation held emergency sessions: virtually all of them deciding to begin evacuating the following day regardless of any progress made by Britain and France in negotiating a settlement with Hitler. That same afternoon special messengers were touring schools delivering instructions: the day and time each school would evacuate. Some authorities even hired vans fitted with loudspeakers to tour round broadcasting arrangements. Children reporting for evacuation were to bring their gas masks, a few clothes and enough food for at least twenty-four hours. Each child should also wear an identity label: some authorities such as Derby issued coloured armbands the colour denoting the school. Teachers would wear a badge with the name of their home town on it.

Manchester's original estimate was for 80,000 children to leave the city accompanied by their teachers. On top of this was a provision for the evacuation of expectant mums, the blind and the physically disabled. Manchester had allowed itself three days to complete the task: special trains were quickly arranged and 140 Corporation buses were taken off scheduled services to help with the city's first full day of evacuations. Dispersal was in all directions with destinations both near and far though as a rule none was to be more than three-and-a-half hours journey time away from home.

The main emphasis for the second day was the evacuation of mothers with children under five years of age, expectant mums and disabled adults. It also involved some schools such as the boys from Manchester Grammar, who went from Victoria, while the girls of Manchester High left from London Road.

On Sunday, schools evacuated included the Central High School for Boys, Chorlton High School and Levenshulme High and eighteen special trains were laid on to carry mothers and young children to places of comparative safety. So successful had Manchester's evacuation plan been that by the time war was declared at 11.00am only nine trains remained to be despatched.

Between 31 August and 8 September 1939 over 1.5 million people were evacuated nation wide. This comprised some 827,000 children, 524,000 mothers and young children, 13,000 expectant mothers, 7,000 handicapped and 103,000 teachers and helpers. Even these figures, impressive though they are and considering that there was not a single serious or fatal accident, were far less than the government had expected. Of the 73,000 children entitled to be evacuated from inner city Birmingham and those areas containing munitions factories, only a third of this number presented themselves on the day. In Sheffield the response was higher with around fifty per cent going but just up the road at Rotherham the figure was a disappointing eight per cent. Less than fifty per cent of children would leave London so that when the Blitz began at least 500,000 youngsters were still living in the metropolitan area. Coventry on the other hand had actually been designated by the government as a place safe from aerial attack and excluded from the general evacuation plan. Only after some serious lobbying from the local authorities was Coventry's overcrowded areas designated evacuable. Last minute plans were cobbled together so that schoolchildren and their teachers could be taken to rural areas around the city such as Kenilworth and Wellesbourne. About half the parents in the approved zones registered with the scheme, the number of children being 8,625 and of these only 3,200 presented themselves when the time came.

Where the children finished up being billeted was anyone's guess. Some slum children finished up in the homes of the wealthy while children from well-to-do families ended up being billeted in slums. One of the better-known stories involves a mother and her toddler who were evacuated from a Glasgow tenement and eventually billeted on a wealthy family in the countryside. As the toddler squatted down in the middle of the drawing room to defecate on an expensive Persian carpet, its mother was quick to admonish the child with words to the effect. "Don't do it on the nice lady's clean carpet. Go and do it in the corner like at home." At the other end of the scale were the six boys who found themselves billeted with the retired colonel of the Durham Light Infantry. He lived in a large house by the river at Romaldkirk and the old boy filled their idle hours by teaching them the rudiments of infantry training in his extensive grounds. From the reports it was fun for all concerned. One of the more disgraceful aspects of evacuation began to rear its ugly head the nearer Christmas got. Many wealthy and middle-class families who had taken people in under extreme sufferance were now forcing evacuees out on to the streets so they could free up rooms to entertain friends and family over the festive season. Happy Christmas.

Within a surprisingly short time however, schoolchildren in the nearer evacuation areas began drifting back home of their own volition. What started as a trickle would soon turn into a flood. It was the same story in Manchester, Sheffield, Leeds, Derby, London and so on. As the weeks passed with no bombing, many parents were tempted to have their children back. Soon, so many children had given up that schools reopened though it is true that many did this with less than half their pre-war complement of pupils. The drift back continued throughout the period now known as the 'Phoney War' (though it was anything but phoney if you were at sea or with the RAF) and many schools were back to full strength before the fall of France in April 1940. Despite the return of children in large numbers, there remained a steady stream of evacuees leaving London and the major industrial centre, many having made private arrangements to stay with relatives.

Mothers, many looking apprehensive, look on as their children board a tram on the first leg of their journey.

"I was born in September 1936 and was three when the war started. I was evacuated to Darwen when I was about four. My mam was supposed to get me to the train station with the St George's, Hulme, contingent, but we were late and they had already left. I can remember having my gas mask box and a label fastened to my coat with my name and address. My mam put me on the next train going out with other children who were older than me. My next memory is of being taken around the streets of this "strange place" with a group of grown-ups who were delivering us to houses. I was put with a couple called Taylor. I called them Mamma and Pappa Taylor. They lived in a chippie, but because of rationing the chippie was not open for business. I stayed there a couple of years but used to get very fretful when my mam visited and then left to go home. After two years my mam took me back home."

Edna Oatway (nee Rigby), Langley, Middleton. (Extract from Tom Waghorn's column, MEN 11 April 1998)

Evacuation of another type also took place in the early war years. On 10 June 1940, Benito Mussolini took Italy into the war on the side of Nazi Germany. In doing so he instantaneously made the thousands of Italians living and working in the UK 'enemy aliens.' Putting it bluntly, the War Office panicked. Suddenly the country was awash with Fascists out to stab us in the back. The Press, Labour and Tory alike had a field day whipping up anti-alien hatred, but the truth was that the Fascist sympathisers among the Italians were very much in the minority. Many Italians had been living and working in Britain for twenty, thirty, even forty years, and didn't care for what Mussolini stood for. Many of them had married British spouses and had children, even grandchildren, already serving in our armed forces. Some Italian immigrants had even fought for the British during the Great War and several had been highly decorated. The War Office made no allowances. Male Italians were rounded up regardless of their sympathies and herded into makeshift camps, one of the most notorious being the rat-infested and derelict. Warth Mills at Bury, where sanitation was almost non-existent, the food inedible and the bedding alive with bugs. On 1 July, internees from Warth Mills were among the mixed bag of Germans, Austrians, and Italians found at Liverpool on board Canada-bound liner *Arandora Star*, the Canadians having offered to take 7,000 male internees. The liner (with 1,564 people on board and lifeboats for only 1,000) was seventy-five miles north west of Ireland when she was intercepted by U47 commanded by Korvetkapitan Gunther Prien. Prien, one of the German Navy's leading aces, had already earned his place in the annals of naval warfare for his daring attack on Scapa Flow on 14 October 1939 during which he sank the battleship HMS *Royal Oak*. The *Arandora Star* was torpedoed and went to the bottom taking 743 people with her, of whom 453 were Italian. Her tragic loss did much among ordinary people to generate opposition to the Cabinet's internment policies, even though the Press continued its anti-alien efforts. It was only when further revelations became public, such as the wholesale robbing of 2,550 internees while on board a liner bound for Australia by both the military escort and crew members alike, that the Government were galvanised into action. Responsibility was transferred to the Home Office who called a halt to internment for all except category 'A' Nazis and known Italian Fascist sympathisers.

THE HOME FRONT

As the international situation deteriorated Parliament was recalled on 22 August to 'meet on Thursday next, when the Government proposes to invite both Houses to pass through all its stages the Emergency Powers (Defence) Bill.' Only eleven members of the Commons voted against an Act that had the potential to bestow unprecedented and wide-ranging powers on ministers and senior bureaucrats alike. Defence Regulations could now be issued as Orders in Council without recourse to Parliament. Any violation of a Defence Regulation was deemed to be a strict liability offence punishable by fine, imprisonment, or both. In theory the regulations held precedence over all other laws including Habeas Corpus, as offenders could be detained indefinitely without trial. Under some of the regulations the prosecution no longer had to prove guilt 'beyond reasonable doubt'. The unfortunates appearing up before the beak had to prove their innocence otherwise they were guilty as charged. Various regulations introduced unprecedented powers of stop, search and interrogation as well as the automatic right to enter premises with having first to obtain a search warrant. An order of 22 May 1940 gave Ernest Bevin complete control over persons and property. He was empowered to direct any person to undertake any service he thought fit; the directed person had no say whatsoever as to what wages would be paid, what hours would be worked or what the conditions were. This was followed two months later by Order 1305 that made strikes and lockouts illegal wherever collective bargaining procedures existed between unions and employers.

The only safeguard against any abuse of power by the executive was the fact that all Orders in Council containing Defence Regulations had to be laid before Parliament at the earliest opportunity. Once laid before them, both Houses then had twenty-eight days in which to scrutinise the Order. During that time either House could resolve that a particular Order be annulled: which it duly was.

One of the immediate effects of the declaration of war was the curtailment of all sporting events and the closure of cinemas and theatres: anywhere in fact where large crowds would assemble. In October the Football League was reorganised on a regional basis for the duration. Manchester United had played only three matches when war was declared and now found itself in the Western Division along with Everton, Liverpool, Stoke City, Manchester City, Chester, Wrexham, Port Vale, New Brighton, Crewe Alexandra, Stockport County and Tranmere Rovers. On Saturday 17 February 1940 a crowd of just 1,000 turned up at Old Trafford to watch United put six goals past Birmingham City in a friendly. Interestingly, Birmingham was winning by two goals to one at half time but Carey and McKay scored in quick succession after the interval to put United ahead. Smith (2) and Carey (1) completed Birmingham's misery.

It was not only football that suffered changes. When horse racing was again allowed it was restricted to a limited number of courses because it was considered a waste of fuel to be transporting nags from one end of the country to the other. During 1940 the sport of kings was again briefly suspended and subsequently restricted to just six courses as many had been taken over for other uses such as the course at Derby which had been turned into a heavy anti-aircraft battery site. Cricket struggled on, even though the Oval was requisitioned for the army and Warwickshire's ground became an AFS station. Greyhound racing, introduced from the USA in 1926 and an instant hit with the working-class as they too could own and race dogs was restricted by the blackout regulation: with tracks such as White City, Belle Vue, and Salford allowed just one afternoon meeting a week. The tracks were soon associated with spivs, the black market, dodgy goods and dodgy deals. Tracks were frequently raided by military and civil police, often mounting joint operations: the punters rounded up and subjected to on-the-spot ID checks.

Popular radio shows, many of which were transmitted from North Wales, included Nether Backwash which starred Robb Wilton and Garrison Theatre which featured Jack Warner. Wing Commander Kenneth Horne and stand-up comic corporal Bill Waddington (Coronation Street's Percy Sugden) featured in 'Ack Ack Here Here'. Horne also appeared alongside Squadron Leader Richard 'Stinker' Murdoch and Eric Barker in Much Binding in the Marsh, a comedy set on an RAF station, with Murdoch and Horne often singing duets as 'The Stinkpots'. During a transmission from London of Shipmates Ashore on 30 June 1944, listeners actually heard a V1 explode as it landed close-by.

Much air time was given to dance band music, some favourites being Billy Cotton, Joe Loss, Jack Hylton and Henry Hall. Popular singers were Gracie Fields, Vera Lynn and Ann Shelton. When the American Forces Network went on air, listeners were treated to the big band sounds of Tommy Dorsey, jazz from Benny Carter and the singing talent of Ella Fitzgerald, while Bing Crosby, Bob Hope, Judy Garland and Frank Sinatra fronted a show called Command Performance.

Cinemas and theatres were allowed to reopen on 15 September and among the films on general release at the time was Errol Flynn in The Prince and the Pauper, Gracie Fields in The Show Goes On and Claude Rains and Fay Bainter in White Banners. During the Blitz on London, cinema and theatre audiences were required to remain in their seats. One night while bombs were raining down Tommy Trinder made his way from one theatre to another offering to go on stage and do a ten minute slot. By the time the raiders had left and the all-clear was sounded Trinder had given seventeen separate performances. From the start Trinder went out of his way to entertain service personnel stationed n the UK, and though at times his material could be earthy, it was never crude. In 1943 he was unjustly singled out in the Commons for not having volunteered for overseas with ENSA.

Just four days after the declaration of war, petrol ration books were issued for the first time. By November the Government was warnings garages that forged petrol coupons were already in circulation. Some of the ways of circumventing petrol rationing was, one, drive off without paying and, two, steal it from the armed forces. This latter activity got so bad that from May 1940 military fuel was dyed and random checks of the contents of private motorists' fuel tanks introduced.

In January 1940, sugar, bacon and butter went on ration, but as many working-class people couldn't afford butter in the first place and could rarely afford bacon the country was awash with the stuff and so double rations were issued. For those unable to afford butter sixpence would buy a pound of margarine (made from whale oil with added vitamins). The weekly allowance per person was two ounces of tea (none for the under fives), two ounces each of butter, sweets and fats, and four ounces each of margarine and sugar. Extra cheese was issued to workers with no canteen facilities and a special ration was organised for vegetarians but they had to surrender their meat coupons. Prime cuts of meat were rationed at six ounces per person per day, though people were free to buy larger quantities of cheap cuts up to cash value of six ounces of prime beef, mutton or pork.

Under the Defence Regulations it was illegal for shopkeepers to sell rationed goods without coupons. Shopkeepers were deliberately targeted by the Food Office, which sent in undercover operatives whose sole purpose was to persuade the shopkeeper to part with a rationed item – such as a packet of butter – without receiving a coupon in exchange. The operatives were at liberty to try any hard luck story they cared to come up with and to persevere until the shopkeeper either handed over the goods or refused point blank. Any shopkeeper falling for a hard luck story was then prosecuted under the regulations. As it was a strict liability offence the shopkeeper was guilty as charged.

Shopkeepers and traders took their used coupons to the Post Office who then issued a voucher, which could then be set against their next wholesale purchase. The regulations required that the used coupons be returned to the appropriate issuing office where they would be checked. This proved to be totally unworkable. Millions and millions of coupons were sloshing about the country every day with no security system in place. The Ministry of Food kept up the pretence that all were checked whereas in reality only a small percentage ever could be. Of course the underworld and unscrupulous retailers alike had rumbled the ministry from the very beginning. The Post Office, responsible for collection and shipment of coupons were overwhelmed almost immediately and modified the system in order to cope. They refused to check or count the coupons handed in and traders were allowed to take in their bundles, which they simply signed for. The unscrupulous trader got his voucher and in return the Ministry got a bundle of coupon-sized newspaper clippings or blank paper bearing a bogus name and address. In 1942 the Ministry of Food finally admitted that thousands of coupons were going adrift every day.

Other targets for the Food Office were cafes and restaurants. Under the regulations it was a strict liability offence to serve a customer with more than two courses, though it wasn't illegal for a customer to pay for their two course meal, leave the restaurant, then come back in, sit at a different table and order two more courses. The meal-snooper's task was to persuade staff into giving them a larger meal than permitted. Not only was the restaurant automatically guilty, so too was the poor waiter or waitress. British restaurants do not appear to have attracted too much attention from the Food Office.

These establishments had set menus and guaranteed the customer a decent meal at a set price. Two were opened on Trafford Park. One was at the rear of the Trafford Park hotel, the other on the corner of Ashburton and Richmond Roads.

On 27 September 1940 Sir John Simon introduced an emergency budget increasing the duty on whisky, tobacco and sugar; the effect of the latter being to drive up prices on a whole range of commodities including tinned fruit, syrup, marmalade, jam and sweetened milk. The 1940 Budget raised the largest sum ever achieved to that date from one year's taxation – a massive £1,234 million out of estimated expenditure of £2,667 million. Income tax was raised from 7/- to 7/6d in the pound and surtax levied on all incomes in excess of £1,500 a year. Beer went up by a penny a pint, whisky by an outrageous 1/9d a bottle, tobacco by three pence an ounce, and matches by a halfpenny a box. Some items such as tinned salmon, crab, oranges, pineapples and fresh lemons were never rationed because supplies virtually dried up. Trade in tinned fish, tinned fruit, tinned rice, ground nut oil, cooking fat, and sugar flourished on the black market as did that for silk stockings, cloth, cosmetics, underwear and shoes. There was always a ready market for additional ration books, for as the war progressed, they rapidly became an alternative form of currency. The longer the books were valid the better the price they commanded. There are cases on record where thieves stole entire stocks from Food Offices; one of the biggest was at Romford in May 1944 when 100,000 books were taken.

In February 1942 Sir Stafford Cripps told the Commons that 'personal extravagance must be eliminated altogether.' Many of Cripps' colleagues found the man, well more than a bit weird. A strict vegetarian, Cripps rose at four every morning, exercised and then took a cold bath. His elimination of personal extravagance translated to no petrol for pleasure motoring, a cut in the clothing ration (introduced during 1941) and sports events curtailed to save fuel. Cigarettes were not on ration but many tobacconists would often sell only to their regular customers. Silk stockings became a thing of the past for many women who were forced to resort to staining their legs with gravy browning. During 1938 Britain had imported 33 million pairs of stockings but by 1944 it would be less than one million. Mind you, the Yanks made up some of the shortfall. Manchester was the centre of one of the biggest clothing coupon forgery scams of the entire war.

The crime of the season in February 1942 was waste. The following month the Paper Order became law making it a crime punishable by a fine of £100 or three months in prison to throw away or destroy a used bus or tram ticket or cigarette packet. Herbert Morrison, Minister of Supply, underlined the announcement saying: "Every piece of paper, every old bone, every piece of scrap metal is a potential bullet against Hitler. We would never fling away a bullet. We must never fling away one piece of scrap that can be salvaged. In this matter men and women in the home have a duty as vital as the men and women in the arms works." All local authorities with populations of more than 10,000 were required to arrange efficient systems of collection and disposal. All householders in those areas were required to co-operate.

The ubiquitous British Railways' sandwich, for several decades the butt of many a joke, finally met its match in November 1939 when it became one of the first casualties of rationing. Despite millions of the wretched things being sold every year, it was announced that they would soon be disappearing from railway refreshment rooms nation wide. Passengers were told that there was nothing to worry about. An assurance was given that the travelling public would not be going hungry. Soon they would be treated to the delights of the British Railways' beef sandwich. Of course it never happened.

The Fuel & Lighting Order came into effect on 7 September 1939: its aim being to reduce total quarterly consumption of electricity to 75per cent of the amount used in the quarter ending 30 June 1939. Twelve days later it was announced that coal rationing would start on 1 October. Householders were required to register with a licensed coal merchant and would then to be advised by a local official as to their basic quantity entitlement for each quarter. The domestic ration was then fixed at around 75 per cent of the basic quantity.

In a way it was a good job that during the first month or two of 1940 we were still in the 'Phoney War' stage of the conflict as severe weather conditions played havoc with road, rail and canal transport. Here troops help clear the LNER route between Manchester and Sheffield.

Though not photographed at Manchester, this Battle for Fuel coach certainly did the rounds of Manchester stations. Visitors were given tips on how to save coal, electricity and gas. For example baths should only be filled to the ankle – and the water should be shared – though its unlikely they were advocating bathing with a friend. The slogan was: 'Less hot water in the bath – More hot water for Hitler.'

One of the many ways of varying diet during the war was by keeping bottled fruit. In some places communal fruit-preserving clubs were formed where residents pooled their resources – fruit, jars, time – and divided the spoils between themselves. Communal jam-making clubs were organised by the WVS.

Comedian and a regular star on BBC radio's *Workers' Playtime*, Robb 'the day war broke out' Wilton, was doing his bit for the war effort by putting in appearances around the Midlands and North West at such events as Food for Victory exhibitions.

MINISTRY  OF FOOD

REGISTER NOW
FOR
MEAT

YOU must register now to enable the Ministry of Food to distribute meat fairly to the shops throughout the country, and to assure YOU of your fair share when rationing begins.

WHAT YOU HAVE TO DO NOW :—

1 Put your name and address on the counterfoil at the bottom of the Meat Page of your Ration Book NOW.

2 Write on the inside front cover of your Ration Book the name and address of your butcher.

3 Take your Ration Book to your butcher and let him write his name and address on the meat counterfoil and cut it out.

4 If you move to another district, take your Ration Book to the local Food Office in your new district.

5 The numbered coupons *must not* be cut out yet. This will be done by your butcher when you do your shopping after meat rationing begins.

6 If you have registered for meat before Christmas, this registration was unauthorised. You may let it stand, and it will then be effective. Or, if you wish, you may register now with another butcher by recovering the counterfoil from the butcher who holds it and taking it to the butcher you now choose.

YOU ARE FREE TO CHOOSE ANY BUTCHER YOU LIKE

YOU MUST REGISTER NOT LATER THAN

MONDAY 8TH JANUARY

AN ANNOUNCEMENT BY THE MINISTRY OF FOOD, GT. WESTMINSTER HOUSE, LONDON, S.W.1

One way of supplementing official rations was by 'growing your own.' Allotments sprang up almost everywhere, school playing fields, waste ground, even on railway embankments. Sixteen acres of land adjacent to the Ford Merlin engine plant at Trafford Park was taken over by the factory and used for growing vegetables for use in the works canteen. Being able to grow your own took on an importance all of its own when the Acquisition of Food (Excessive Quantities) Order came into force. Officials were given powers to enter homes and inspect the contents of the larder. If there was more than a week's ration of any item on ration – even by the smallest amount – the householder faced prosecution, a fine and possible imprisonment. Bureaucratic eccentricity reached even newer heights when it was decreed that bread could no longer be served in cafes and restaurants at lunchtime. Notices appeared in all seriousness in the press announcing the fact that Food Office officials would be mounting lightning raids on eating establishments to see what diners had on their side plates.

Ladies from the WVS sow potatoes on an area of waste ground.

Government regulations required farmers, smallholders, even householders to register livestock, it being a serious offence not to. Notification also had to be given of any animal sent for slaughter as well as any that had died from any other cause. Farms were subject to spot visits by officials who made sure that the figures tallied. Every piece of meat destined for butchers' shops was counted and weighed under the watchful eye of a government inspector before it left the wholesale market. One farmer who had managed to rear a pig without it being registered almost got away with it. His mistake was in having it killed along with a registered pig because he then sent two left sides to the wholesale market. Rabbits, pigeon and freshwater fish became far game for those finding the meat ration inadequate, and many a cat ended its days being passed off as a freshly skinned rabbit by butchers out to make a few extra bob.

Forty city girls from Manchester recruited for the Women's Land Army, which was mobilised to keep the country's food production going while young farmers were away fighting. A surprising number of WLA members got to like the work so much that many of them stayed in farming after the war.

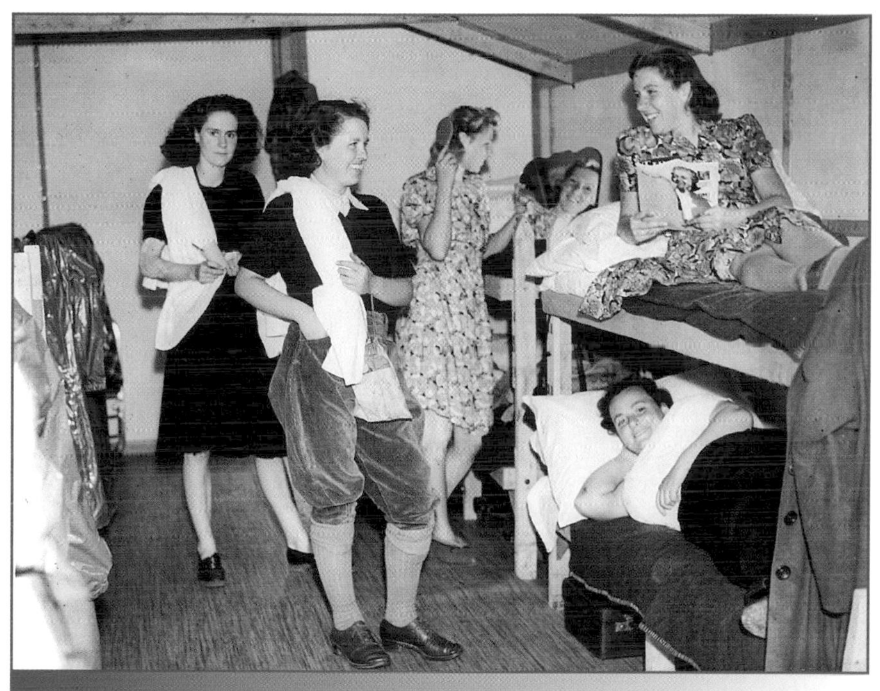

Rest and relaxation time at a Women's Land Army hostel in July 1941. These particular girls came from different parts of the country including Manchester, St Albans, Cheltenham and Norwich. None of them came from an immediate farming background. They worked on marked gardens within a three-mile radius of the hostel.

Members of the Women's Land Army get a taste of life under canvas.

FOOD FACTS

Frugal but Festive

It will take more than Hitler to stop the British housewife from setting a festive table at Christmas time. Yes, the food will be the same—rations, vegetables, grain foods—no Christmas specials; because ship-saving matters more than ever now we have gone over to the offensive. But by dressing up the old favourites, by using little tricks of flavouring, garnishing and serving we can still put up a festive show. Stuffed flank of beef may take the place of turkey, and a little cold tea may be used to darken the complexion of Christmas cake or pudding, but we can still contrive a spread which will delight the children and warm the hearts of the grown-ups.

FOR FATHER — CHRISTMAS DAY PUDDING

Rub 3 oz. cooking fat into 6 tablespoonfuls of flour until like fine crumbs. Mix in 1½ breakfastcupfuls of stale breadcrumbs, 1 lb. prunes (soaked 24 hours, stoned, chopped) or any other dried fruit such as sultanas, 3 oz. sugar, 1 teaspoonful mixed spice, ½ teaspoonful grated nutmeg. Then chop 1 large apple finely, grate 1 large raw carrot and 1 large raw potato; add to dry ingredients. Stir in 3 reconstituted dried eggs. Mix 1 teaspoonful of bicarbonate of soda in 1 tablespoonful of mixed lemon substitute and stir thoroughly into the pudding mixture. Put into one large or two small well-greased basins, cover with margarine papers and steam 2½ hours. This can be prepared overnight and eaten on Christmas Day.

WITH LOVE TO THE CHILDREN — CHRISTMAS FRUIT PIES

(A good alternative to mincemeat.)

Warm 1 tablespoonful of marmalade (or jam, but this is not so spicy) in small saucepan over tiny heat. Add ½ lb. prunes (soaked 24 hours, stoned, chopped) or other dried fruit, 1 tablespoonful of sugar, 1 teacupful stale cake crumbs, or half cake, half breadcrumbs, ½ teaspoonful mixed spice. Stir together until crumbs are quite moist. Remove from heat, add 1 large chopped apple; also some chopped nuts if possible. Use as a filling for small tarts or pies.

CHILDREN'S TREAT

1 Grated bar chocolate on freshly made biscuits gives the party touch.

2 Baked apples stuffed with war-time mincemeat are a splendid surprise.

3 Hot Cinnamon Toast for tea makes up for the shortage of cakes. Here is the way to make it.

Cinnamon Toast

Take 1 tablespoonful margarine, 1 dessertspoonful of sugar, 1 teaspoonful of cinnamon. Cream all the ingredients together, spread on hot toast and grill for two minutes.

THIS IS WEEK 22—THE SECOND WEEK OF RATION PERIOD No. 6 (Dec. 13th to Jan. 9th)

It began in individual homes during the winter of 1939/40 as ladies of all ages and from all walks of life turned to knitting scarves, gloves and balaclavas for service personnel and prisoners of war. By the fall of France, this home industry had blossomed into something quite different. As younger women either joined the armed forces or went out to work, older ladies took over the task on such a scale that knitting clubs, such as this one organised by a local Conservative Party, were formed all over the country. As the war progressed, a make do and mend siege culture developed. Every ball of wool, every remnant of clothing was utilised: even grandma's old bloomers were recycled. Grown-ups' clothes were cut down for the kids: knitted garments were unpicked and the wool reused time and again.

This five-foot high pile represents just one morning's contribution of socks knitted for the troops.

RATIONING

of Clothing, Cloth, Footwear

from June 1, 1941

Rationing has been introduced, not to deprive you of your real needs, but to make more certain that you get your share of the country's goods—to get fair shares with everybody else.

When the shops re-open you will be able to buy cloth, clothes, footwear and knitting wool *only if you bring your Food Ration Book with you.* The shopkeeper will detach the required number of coupons from the unused margarine page. Each margarine coupon counts as one coupon towards the purchase of clothing or footwear. You will have a total of 66 coupons to last you for a year; so go sparingly. You can buy *where* you like and *when* you like without registering.

NUMBER OF COUPONS NEEDED

Men and Boys	Adult	Child
Unlined mackintosh or cape ..	9	7
Other mackintoshes, or raincoat, or overcoat	16	11
Coat, or jacket, or blazer or like garment	13	8
Waistcoat, or pull-over, or cardigan, or jersey	5	3
Trousers (other than fustian or corduroy)	8	6
Fustian or corduroy trousers ..	5	5
Shorts	5	3
Overalls, or dungarees or like garment	6	4
Dressing-gown or bathing-gown	8	6
Night-shirt or pair of pyjamas ..	8	6
Shirt, or combinations—woollen	8	6
Shirt, or combinations—other material	5	4
Pants, or vest, or bathing costume, or child's blouse	4	2
Pair of socks or stockings ..	3	1
Collar, or tie, or pair of cuffs ..	1	1
Two handkerchiefs	1	1
Scarf, or pair of gloves or mittens	2	2
Pair of slippers or goloshes ..	4	2
Pair of boots or shoes	7	3
Pair of leggings, gaiters or spats	3	2

Women and Girls	Adult	Child
Lined mackintoshes, or coats (over 28 in. in length) ..	14	11
Jacket, or short coat (under 28 in. in length)	11	8
Dress, or gown, or frock—woollen	11	8
Dress, or gown, or frock—other material	7	5
Gym tunic, or girl's skirt with bodice	8	6
Blouse, or sports shirt, or cardigan, or jumper	5	3
Skirt, or divided skirt	7	5
Overalls, or dungarees or like garment	6	4
Apron, or pinafore	3	2
Pyjamas	8	6
Nightdress	6	5
Petticoat, or slip, or combination, or cami-knickers	4	3
Other undergarments, including corsets	3	2
Pair of stockings	2	1
Pair of socks (ankle length) ..	1	1
Collar, or tie, or pair of cuffs ..	1	1
Two handkerchiefs	1	1
Scarf, or pair of gloves or mittens or muff	2	2
Pair of slippers, boots or shoes ..	5	3

CLOTH. Coupons needed per yard depend on the width. For example, a yard of woollen cloth 36 inches wide requires 3 cou…

KN…

THESE GOODS M…

¶Children's clothing of siz… and workmen's bib and brace… mending silk. ¶Boot and sho… in width. ¶Elastic. ¶Lace … ¶Hard haberdashery. ¶Clogs…

Special Notice

Retailers will be allowed … other rationed goods up to … COUPONS. After those da… their customers' coupons. S… limit during these periods th… manufacturer to any one retai… *from your Trade Organisation…*

ISSUED …

MINISTRY OF SUPPLY

RUBBER SHORTAGE

GO EASY WITH YOUR TYRES

HOW FAST DRIVING WASTES RUBBER

Miles Per Hour	RUBBER WASTED
30	NORMAL WEAR
40	WASTAGE INCREASED BY 1/4
50	WASTAGE INCREASED BY OVER 1/3
60	WASTAGE INCREASED BY OVER 1/2
70	WASTAGE INCREASED BY NEARLY 3/4

90% of the world's natural rubber resources are in enemy hands — care in the use of tyres is the most effective way to conserve the nation's available supplies.

Have tyre pressures checked every week. Submit tyres for replacement before the fabric is visible. Never drive a commercial vehicle above its legal speed limit. Avoid driving a car over 40 m.p.h. Never corner at speed. See that wheels are in proper alignment. Never accelerate fiercely. Remember that fierce braking wastes rubber.

Worn-out tyres and tubes are wanted immediately. Take *yours* to a local Garage for despatch to a Government Depot. Or put them out for collection by the Local Authority; or sell them to a Merchant.

SALVAGE STEWARDS ARE WANTED. If you can help, apply to your Local Authority; and so do your bit towards increasing the collection, not only of **RUBBER**, but also of **PAPER, METAL, RAGS, BONES, KITCHEN WASTE.**

"I set her up on HALL'S WINE"

Think of the satisfaction expressed in those few words! They were actually overheard in a Glasgow restaurant. The truth is Hall's Wine overcomes exhaustion by giving the blood *new life.* First, Hall's Wine is a natural life-force, created by nature's own fusion of more than thirty active elements. Then Hall's Wine is specially medicated to enrich your blood, and to help your blood enrich itself—for your *lasting* strength. Buy a bottle of Hall's Wine today, and you will possess the secret of real recovery this very day.

Hall's Wine

From Wine Merchants, Grocers and Chemists with Wine Licences. Large bottle 6/6; Smaller size 3/9. Stephen Smith & Co. Ltd., Bow, London, E.3.

(332)

HALL'S WINE The Tonic Builder

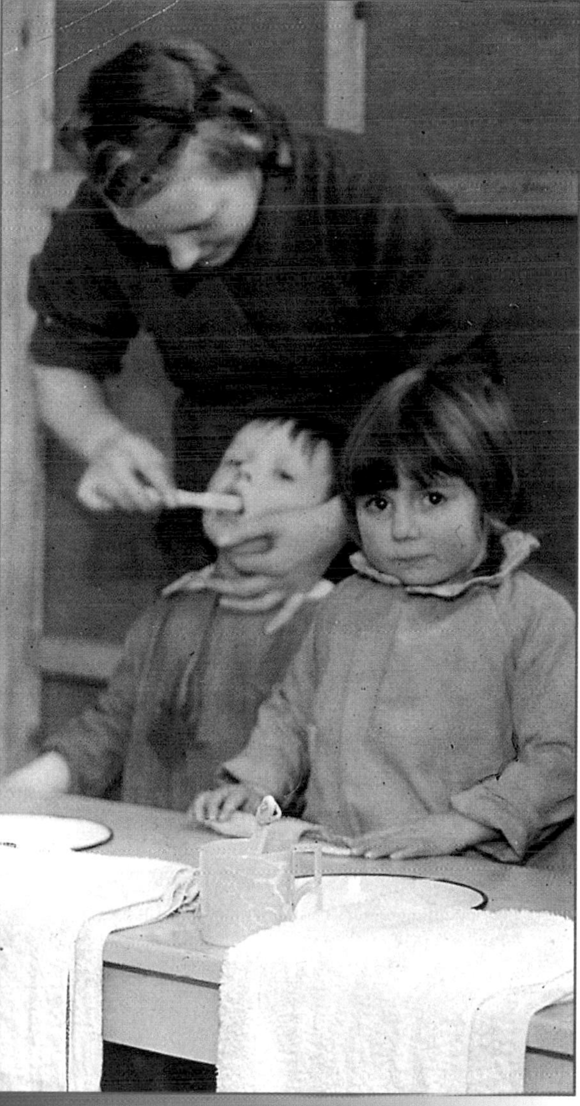

With more and more young women taking up jobs in the munitions industries and so on, it was found that provision had to be made for the care of their young children while they were out at work. Not everyone had adult relatives around to take on the job. To overcome the problem a system of day nurseries was soon established.

'Papers please!' A woman shows her identity card to a Home Guardsman on duty outside the Co-op headquarters in Corporation Street. This image is in fact a still from the historic footage shot by the Manchester-based Co-operative Wholesale Society film unit during the Blitz. Though formed primarily to make publicity films, the unit was transformed almost overnight into documentary filmmakers as they graphically recorded the events of December 1940. The fifteen-minute film lay forgotten for almost fifty years until 1989 when it was shown at the British Film Institute as part of an exhibition celebrating fifty years of British cinema. Local interest was such that the film was put on continuous showing at the Greater Manchester Museum of Science and Industry, Castlefield.

The *Manchester Guardian* offices on Cross Street during the dark days of the war. The word 'Manchester' has been stripped off the front of the building as a security measure.

The role of Belle Vue during the war cannot be underestimated as it played a vital part in the 'Holidays at Home' campaign. It was one of the only venue's of its kind to stay open during the war years, although many of the rides were closed and the popular firework displays were cancelled. Belle Vue opened its grounds and exhibition halls for training purposes for the military.

The Free Trade Hall played host to many conferences and speakers. In this photograph, Winston Churchill addresses the audience in January 1940. By December of that same year the building was demolished in the Christmas Blitz.

Perched on the back of an old car, Winston Churchill stops to share a joke on his way through Chorlton. 1941.

Winston Churchill took advantage of a public speech he made in Manchester on 27 January 1940 to berate the Government for not expanding industry quickly enough now that the country was at war. Despite the fact that war had been declared on 3 September 1939, there were still over one million people on the dole. A number of centres were opened to address skills shortages. They were open to unemployed men and women alike.

Unemployed men hoping for work in aeroplane manufacturing learn some basic skills at one of the special centres.

The Avro Anson, of which 11,000 would eventually be built, was developed from an order placed by Imperial Airways for a couple of small, twin-engined monoplane airliners that might also find gainful employment carrying mail. The design was the Avro 652 and both machines were delivered during 1935. As luck would have it the Air Ministry was shopping around for a light coastal patrol aircraft and by chance the Avro 652 almost matched the specification. Avro's design genius Roy Chadwick came up with the required modifications which included a mid-upper turret to create the Avro Anson. The rest is history. From March 1939 Avro began transferring workers from Newton Heath to the new factory at Chadderton, where the first aircraft to be put into production was the Bristol Blenheim, Avro having been awarded a contract to build 250. Construction of the Anson was transferred to a plant at Yeadon Airport (now Leeds/Bradford) and production peaked at 135 aircraft a month. Ansons were used in all manner of roles including maritime reconnaissance, anti-submarine, light bomber, training and communications, while the Mark XI was given a deeper fuselage and increased headroom so that it could operate as an air ambulance.

This often-produced photograph was taken on 21 December 1940 at Metrovicks, Trafford Park. It is of the test assembly of the first of one hundred Avro Manchester heavy bombers scheduled to be constructed by the company. As Trafford Park lacked a runway it was impossible to fly out completed aircraft so it was decided that the planes would be delivered to the Avro plant at Woodford for final assembly. This plane (R5768) was put together to make sure Metrovicks had got it right after which it was to be dismantled and sent in sections to Woodford. Ironically even before R5768 had been put together the decision to abandon the twin-engined Manchester in favour of the four-engined Lancaster bomber had already been taken. Even more ironic is that two nights after this picture was taken R5768 and components for the next twelve Manchesters were destroyed in the Christmas Blitz. The Manchester bomber was not a success in squadron service: it was beset with technical problems, mainly caused by its Rolls-Royce Vulture engines. During the whole of December 1940 the six Manchesters of 207 Squadron clocked up just seventy-eight flying hours between them. But when it did fly, the Manchester provided RAF Bomber Command with some real hitting power - it was the only bomber capable of carrying the 4,000lb 'Cookie' bomb, and its maximum payload of 10,350lb was greater than any other heavy until early 1942.

TEAM WORK TELLS

Get together and
form a War Savings Group
in your firm today

Every business organisation is asked to form a War Savings Group now. It's easy to arrange. So get one going amongst your fellow-workers, or tell your boss "We want to start a Savings Group right away."
Group Savings begin earning interest immediately. They provide for your future, and for your country's security. They give your country the might and the power to hasten the end of the war.

Apply to your local Savings Committee or to the National Savings Committee, London, S.W.1.

LEND TO DEFEND THE RIGHT TO BE FREE
ISSUED BY THE NATIONAL SAVINGS COMMITTEE

The Metrovicks aircraft factory after the Christmas Blitz.

Damage done to the Metrovicks plant during the Christmas Blitz put aircraft production back by nearly six months, though by March 1942 the company had completed forty-three Manchesters before switching production fully to the output of Lancasters. As early as May 1941 Metrovicks had begun tooling up for the heavy, the first being scheduled for completion during January 1942. As with the Manchester, Lancasters were sent in sections to Woodford for final assembly. In all Metrovicks built 1,080 Lancasters as well as supplying undercarriage assemblies to other manufacturers within the Lancaster Group of companies. The firm also supplied spares for a further 63 Lancasters and undercarriage assemblies for Halifax bombers.

Members of the Avro experimental work force who were based at Ringway.

Designed as a light bomber, the prototype Fairey Battle first flew on 10 March 1936 and deliveries to operational squadrons began the following year. Fitted with the Rolls-Royce Merlin II, a variable pitch propeller and retractable undercarriage, the all-metal Battle was a state-of-art aircraft when first produced. However its front-line career was to be short-lived as rapid advances in fighter plane development overtook it. Too slow and armed with only two 7.69mm machineguns, the Battle stood little chance against the Luftwaffe's highly manoeuvrable and well-armed Me109s and Focke Wolfe 190s. All was not lost, however, as the Battle's large cockpit made it ideal for use as a trainer and large numbers were transferred to the Empire Training Scheme. A total of 2,419 were built and the Fleet Air Arm briefly tested one.

The Fairey Fulmar was developed to provide the Fleet Air Arm with a modern carrier-based fighter with firepower similar to that of the RAF's Hurricanes and Spitfires. The prototype was first flown from Ringway on 4 January 1940 and was later transferred to the A&AEE unit at Boscombe Down for further tests. At the same time the second prototype was delivered to No778 Squadron FAA at Lee on Solent. During June 1940, No778 and front-line squadrons No803 and No806 began receiving Fulmars in large numbers. A few months later No806 Squadron embarked on the carrier *Illustrious*. The Heaton Chapel factory turned out 600 and all were flown at Ringway. The aircraft, which was powered by the 1,300hp Rolls-Royce Merlin XXX, was capable of a top speed of 273mph and had a ceiling of 27,230ft. Mark II Fulmars were modified for operations in the tropics and a number also operated in the night-fighter role. The aircraft's general lack of speed saw it withdrawn from the front-line during late 1942 to early 1943, though it continued in use as a trainer for pilots destined to fly the Barracuda. The Barracuda was a three-seat torpedo/bomber/reconnaissance plane of which 2,572 were built the orders split between Fairey, Blackburn, Boulton Paul, and Westland. The Mark IIs and Mark IIIs flew with the 1,640hp Rolls-Royce Merlin 32 in-line engine: the Mark Is with the 1260hp Merlin XXX.

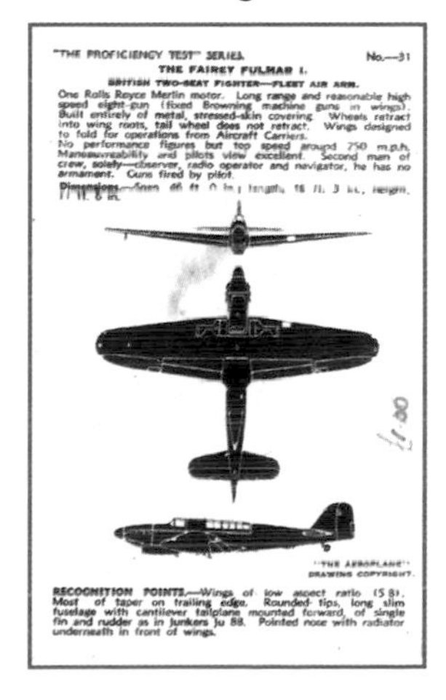

"THE PROFICIENCY TEST" SERIES. No.—31

THE FAIREY FULMAR I.

BRITISH TWO-SEAT FIGHTER—FLEET AIR ARM.

One Rolls Royce Merlin motor. Long range and reasonable high speed eight-gun (fixed Browning machine guns in wings). Built entirely of metal, stressed-skin covering. Wheels retract into wing roots, tail wheel does not retract. Wings designed to fold for operations from Aircraft Carriers.

No performance figures but top speed around 250 m.p.h. Manoeuvreability and pilots view excellent. Second man of crew, solely—observer, radio operator and navigator, he has no armament. Guns fired by pilot.

Dimensions.—Span 46 ft. 0 in.; length, [illegible] ft. 3 in., height, 11 ft. 6 in.

"THE AEROPLANE" DRAWING COPYRIGHT.

RECOGNITION POINTS.—Wings of low aspect ratio (5.8). Most of taper on trailing edge. Rounded tips, long slim fuselage with cantilever tailplane mounted forward, of single fin and rudder as in Junkers Ju 88. Pointed nose with radiator underneath in front of wings.

The prototype Avro transport plane flew from Ringway on 5 July 1942. The York incorporated a number of assemblies from the Lancaster bomber including its wings and tail section. However the York's handling characteristics resulted in the tail design being modified to include a centre fin.

On 22 October 1939 the Ford Motor Co was asked to locate, equip and manage a shadow factory for the mass production of Merlin XX aero engines. Ford's expertise at mass production was urgently required, but it was also vitally important that parts from similar engines built by Rolls Royce or by Packard in the USA should be fully interchangeable. To begin with a part of the old Ford factory at Trafford Park was turned into a tool-room, and machine-tools, technicians and draughtsmen were transferred from Dagenham. Rolls-Royce provided the initial drawings as well as a number of skilled engineers. By September 1940 several buildings had been erected at Eccles and before the year was out 2,300 workers had been hired. However when Ford started recruiting its workforce it had difficulty in attracting skilled workers - it is likely that the majority of skilled people were already in employment - so it had to rely on untrained men, youths and women. Even so the first test Merlin rolled off the production line just a few weeks later.

The first production Merlins were delivered in June 1941 at a cost of £5,640 each, with regular deliveries to aircraft manufacturers commencing two months later. In March 1942 the Air Ministry asked Ford to step up production from 400 to 600 engines a month plus fourteen per cent in spares. By this date productivity was such that the book price of Merlins had fallen to £2,484 each. By April 1944 production was running at 900 engines per month. The workforce had grown to 17,307 of which 5,828 were women.

In June 1940 the BBC aired the first *Workers' Playtime*, a variety show broadcast from a works 'somewhere in England'. The early programmes followed a set format: piano medley, a culture slot featuring a tenor or soprano, and finishing off with a comedian and a bit of a sing along. Bill Gates was the compère and regular acts included comedy turns from Harry Champion, Billy Kaye, Tony Fame, Robb Wilton, Elsie and Doris Waters and Claude Dampier. The show was an instant success, so much so that form October 1940 it went to three shows a week. Shift workers were catered for from June 1942 with a midnight broadcast that was also transmitted to the USA. The BBC didn't always get things right, though. On 11 November 1941, the organisation broadcast loyal birthday greetings to the King of Italy, a country we had been at war with for the best part of eighteen months.

CANTEEN SERVICE

The new CANTEEN will be OPEN MONDAY NEXT, SEPT. 29th.

Those wishing to have Dinners on that day should purchase their tickets from the Canteen on Saturday Sept. 27th

The following prices will be Charged in the Canteen

Meat 2 Vegetables, Bread		10d & 11d
Fish " "		10d
Boiled Pudding & Cutard		3d
Milk " "		3d
Stewed Fruit "		3d
Cakes		1½d & 2d
Tea	per ½ pint	1d
Coffee or Cocoa	"	1½d

Employees should note that they are expected to provide their own Knife, Fork & Spoon

Barrage balloons being manufactured at Dunlop's Manchester factory. Some of the balloons have been partially inflated to allow workers to check the seams for leaks. Each balloon held around 19,000cubic feet of highly flammable hydrogen gas when fully inflated and measured approximately 63ft x 31ft.

A rail-mounted 2,500Kw mobile power station built by Metrovicks for the USSR awaits loading at the docks. Each unit consisted of a power truck with turbine, condenser and alternator.

A Ferranti-built mobile transformer awaits dispatch from their works. They were designed so that limited power supplies could be quickly restored to bombed areas.

As early as 1936 locomotive builders Beyer Peacock & Co, Gorton, were asked if they would be able to manufacture 1,000ib bomb cases should the need arise. Companies such as Beyer Peacock, Vulcan Foundry, and the North British Locomotive Co were ideal candidates for manufacturing munitions as their works were equipped with foundries, machine shops, erecting shops and so on. They also had highly skilled draughtsmen and workers. The following year the company was approached to build gun carriages and mountings for various pieces of ordnance including 12pdr naval guns, anti-aircraft guns, and 9.2inch howitzers. During July 1940 Beyer Peacock became involved in the Vauxhall Motors led A22 tank project. Gorton was to be responsible for constructing the hulls and other components as well as the final assembly. Taylor Bros., Trafford Park was also involved in the A22 project, forging the steel tracks. The tank is better known to most of us as the Churchill and this picture is of a Mark 7 flame-thrower variant.

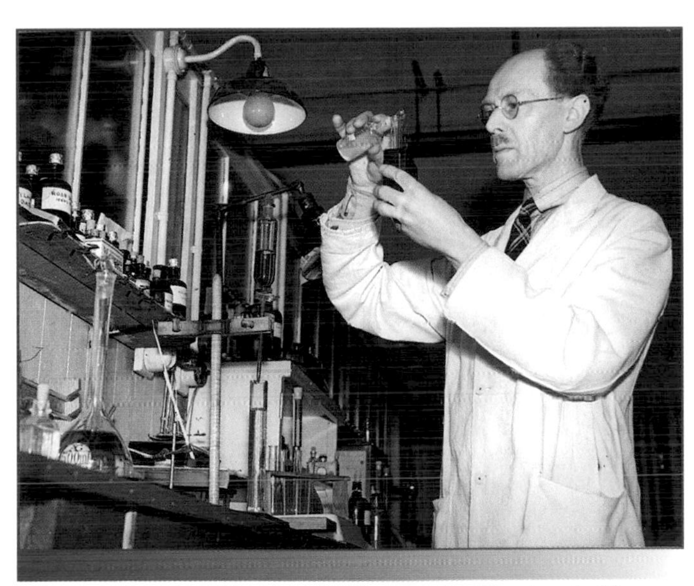

ICI were involved in developing synthetic dyestuffs that could be used in uniforms andacutecamouflage. The company operated the first facility in the UK for the mass production of penicillin.

The war effort was about more than just turning out guns, tanks, planes and ships. In these pictures we see canvas covers being made for use on army vehicles, and women assembling binoculars from supplied components.

Air Raid Precautions & Civil Defence

The war is just five days old and the frontage of the P & O shipping office in Cockspur Street is being sandbagged. The Air Raid Shelter signs denote that P & O House had been designated a public shelter. Before the large surface shelters - such as those in Piccadilly Gardens - were built, local authorities were still required to provide shelter accommodation in town centres. The government ordered all authorities to survey all existing cellars and vaults within town centres to access suitability and to undertake any remedial work necessary.

Surface shelters made from sandbags cover much of Albert Square.

Some of the surface shelters – each capable of holding 200 people – that were erected in Piccadilly Gardens. Built of brick and concrete, they were larger versions of the communal surface shelters built in the streets in residential areas. Many lacked proper ventilation and any form of sanitation, though even those equipped with the luxury of a chemical toilet stank. The long arm of the Defence Regulations even stretched to behaviour in public shelters. Poor George Hall was jailed for fourteen days for snoring during an air raid as he 'did wilfully disturb other persons in the proper use of an air raid shelter'. George's defence that he couldn't be held responsible for his behaviour when asleep was thrown out.

This picture, dating from summer 1940, shows some of the brick-built surface shelters in Piccadilly Gardens. However, in the distance behind the group of people is what appears to be one of the shelters that were constructed from sandbags. By the end of 1940 rumours were circulating nation-wide that many surface shelters were little more than brick coffins having been thrown up by cowboy builders. Rumour turned to fact during the London Blitz when a shelter in McFarlane Lane, Hammersmith, collapsed on its occupants with fatal consequences. Hammersmith's Clerk of Works and the building contractor were arrested on charges of corruption and only narrowly escaped being charged with murder. No less than 120 shelters in Hammersmith had to be torn down and rebuilt.

The fact that 75 tons of pig iron as been balanced on top of the Anderson shelter is not quite as loony as it might first appear. The shelter was in fact being put through a series of load bearing tests to see how much weight the structure could take before it buckled. The engineers believed it would have carried up to 125 tons.

Named after Sir John Anderson, Secretary of State for Home Affairs, the Anderson became a familiar sight at the bottom of many a garden and thousands of examples still survive sixty years after the end of the war. By the end of October 1939 approximately 2,250,000 Andersons had been distributed free of charge, but a change in Government policy resulted in people whose earnings were more than £5 a week having to buy their own at prices ranging from £6.14s to £10.18s. These shelters were cheap to produce. They consisted of two corrugated steel walls that met in a ridge at the top. These were then bolted on to sturdy rails to give the structure strength. Ideally the shelter was then 'planted' three feet into the ground and the remaining exposed sides top covered with at least eighteen inches of compacted earth. When the instructions were adhered to these shelters proved surprisingly robust and could survive almost anything save a direct hit from a bomb. In London a family of three emerged shaken but otherwise unharmed after a shot down Messerschmitt Bf109 had crashed on top of their Anderson.

Manchester Corporation's Crossley-built trolleybus No1000 is seen here equipped with hooded lights and white-painted fenders so that it could be operated during the blackout. The headlights of military, public service and commercial vehicles were fitted with bulbs that gave out quite a low light and even this was deflected downwards by means of slotted covers. Bus and tram windows were usually fitted with heavy black pull-down curtains, though some authorities simply painted over them. By November 1939 so many accidents were occurring during the blackout that a new maximum speed limit of 20mph was imposed. It was to be enforced by police patrol cars cruising along at 20mph waiting to be overtaken – the first man to be convicted of exceeding the new limit was caught doing 34mph in a hearse. Winston Churchill wrote to the Prime Minister suggesting that it might be better if we adopted the 'dim-out' that the French were using, which left visibility at around 600yards. Churchill also highlighted the fact that people were being prosecuted for even the most minor infringement of the regulations, including a man fined for smoking a cigarette too brightly. He also pointed out that the blackout increased the menace of criminal assault, something that proved all too true.

In the first weeks of the war many people objected to being told to 'put that bloody light out!'. If an aircraft was heard overhead people would come out and have a look – they wanted to see what was going on.

The blackout shutters are rolled back at Metrovicks to allow in a little extra light.

Black-Out Tomorrow: 4.35 p.m.

SUMMER-TIME ends at 3 a.m. tomorrow, and from next week the black-out will descend on Britain an hour earlier. The clock goes BACK.

Many offices and warehouses are planning to close earlier, but, even so, workers will have to go home in the black-out.

The departure of B.S.T. is regretted by shopkeepers and business men, but farmers and others who have to start work early in the day welcome the return of G.M.T. Shopkeepers deplore the change (see Page Nine).

Make note of the revised black-out times :

Tonight 5.36*—6.55a.m.†
Tomorrow 4.35†—6.57 a.m.†

* Summer Time
† Winter Time

With mashing cans at the ready workers take cover in an underground shelter.

As an ARP measure, scrap metal specialists George Cohen & Co of Sheffield were called in during October 1940 to dismantle Metrovicks' distinctive water tower as it was considered too much of a landmark to leave standing. The structure, over 200ft tall, was reduced to a height of fifty feet. The rump was then used as an anti-aircraft gun platform.

This Guardian picture dated 13 August 1941, shows a warden and a messenger boy wearing the new (1941 pattern) ARP dark blue dress uniform. It later became standard issue for most Civil Defence workers.

Salford ARP wardens and ARP messenger boys pose for the camera.

Members of the Eccles ARP service.

For several months, the bombed-out areas of Piccadilly presented the ARP services with an ideal training ground where various rescue and decontamination procedures could be tried out. A major exercise held in May 1941 assumed that as well as high explosives and incendiaries, Manchester had also been attacked with gas bombs. Here a heavy rescue squad come to grips with the practicalities of erecting and using shear legs whilst wearing full anti-gas protective clothing.

One element of the May exercise required a decontamination squad to spread bleach powder to counteract the effects of gas. Another important unit within the ARP structure was the Gas Identification Squad. Recruited from qualified chemists, their job was to identify the various types of gas that might be dropped by the Luftwaffe – lung irritants, blister gases, tear gas, etc. The method for dealing with blister gas – which showed up as a dark splash on skin and clothes alike – was to dab, not wipe off the skin and then rub in No2 anti-gas ointment or bleach cream onto the offending parts. Failing that the treatment was to wash immediately in warm water. Clothes could be decontaminated simply by washing them.

Even toddlers at day nursery schools had to take part in gasmask drills. Initially gasmasks simply came in large, medium and small sizes. The coloured 'Mickey Mouse' respirators for children came later as did respirators for babies. Baby respirators were like carrycots with a canopy over. The main problem was that the baby's air supply was by means of a hand operated pump.

An AFS (Auxiliary Fire Service) messenger boy in full anti-gas kit. In October 1939 members of Manchester AFS were becoming disgruntled over their rates of pay. They were paraded by the Chief Constable and threatened with imprisonment if they attempted any form of industrial action.

AFS crews training with various trailer pumps at St Josephs. A pair of AFS heavy painted in battleship grey can be seen at left in the rear background. Heavy pumps were mounted on skids with self-contained engines and were capable of supplying 750 gallons per minute through four delivery valves. A number of different vehicle chassis were used, including the Dennis 40-cwt, both the Bedford WL and ML types, Fordson 7V, Morris Commercial and the Austin K4. The Ford V8 engine was chosen to power pumps built by both Tangye and Sulzer, while those built by Gwynne used a Leyland. Realising that the AFS needed something a little pokier, the Home Office placed an order with Gwynne for a number of extra heavy units. They were mounted on the Austin K4 chassis and used a Leyland engine. Pumping capacity was 1,100 gallons per minute through sic delivery valves.

The Co-operative Wholesale Society AFS unit goes into action during the Christmas Blitz. Trailer mounted pumps were mainly manufactured by Coventry Climax, Scammel, Worthington-Simpson, Beresford and Dennis. Large and medium pumps had two delivery valves and a pumping capacity in the range of 250 to 500 gallons per minute. Light pumps, though trailer-mounted, were detachable so that they could if necessary be manhandled over rubble and debris or taken into a confined space. They had one delivery valve and pumped between 150 and 170 gallons per minute. The smallest was the wheelbarrow pump, designed specifically for use in confined spaces and capable of being carried by one man.

The King and Queen take time out to chat with nurses attending the ARP services parade at Chetham's Hospital in February 1941.

National Fire Service dispatch riders Jessie Harding (left) and Edna Slack.

Sir Felix Pole chats with members of the Metrovicks NFS unit.

Volunteers man one of the thousands of Royal Observer Corps Posts that were spread across the country. Their task was to track and report enemy raiders and friendly aircraft alike.

Twenty Chain Home radar stations made up the front line of Britain's early warning system against high-altitude bombers and were placed at intervals from Netherbutton on the East Coast to Ventnor on the Isle of Wight. A further system of Chain Home Low stations to detect low-flying aircraft was commissioned in July 1940. Once radar had detected bombers, say, south of the French coast, the RAF had about seventeen minutes in which to scramble its interceptors to 20,000ft. Once past the radar station footprints, it often fell to the Royal Observer Corps posts to track and report; their messages were then relayed to ARP control centres, anti-aircraft commands and the appropriate RAF Group. A notebook kept by Eric Green of Ambergate, Derbyshire, records the following for December 1940. 'Incident 76 December 22, enemy activity from 6.30 to 6.30 (12hrs night), Manchester. Anti-aircraft gunfire heard. Incident 77 December 23, enemy aircraft 4.10 to 4.30 (20 min daylight), Midlands. Incident 78, December 23, enemy activity from 7.00 to 12.00 (5 hours night), Manchester. Anti-aircraft gunfire heard. Incident 79, December 23, enemy activity from 1.00 to 1.20 (20 min morning), Midlands.' Eric also recorded the V1 attack on Manchester as 'Incident 146, 24 December 1944, 5.30 to 6.30 (1 hour, morning), Midlands/North West, Flying Bombs.'

Manned by regular troops, these large Haslar mobile smoke generators were deployed to shield industrial complexes from aircraft. The generators - each with a two-man crew - consumed fuel oil and water at rates of about eighty-five and seventy gallons per hour respectively and were usually kept burning for eight to nine hours at a time. By July 1940 eight mobile screens were operational mainly in the north east protecting such places as the ICI chemical plants at Billingham, where, during trials, it was found that plumes of white industrial steam showed above the screen. To get round this problem pitch was added to the mix thereby creating black fumes, which then merged with the steam and smoke from the works to create an effective, if somewhat smelly smoke screen. By the end of 1943 the mobile smoke screen force comprised 500 civilians, 10,000 regular troops and 1,500 generators.

THE BLITZ

In June 1939 the Luftwaffe began a major photo-reconnaissance of the United Kingdom, priority being given to locating and identifying possible industrial, economic, transport and communications targets. Docks, factories, mines, chemical plants, textile mills, railway sidings, bridges, power stations and water and sewage works were individually identified and plotted onto copies of Ordnance Survey maps. Each town was allocated its own distinctive identification number, and every target within that town was also numbered. However the Luftwaffe were not always accurate in their target assessment as they appear to have taken the information printed on Ordnance Survey maps as gospel. Fine if the map in question is up to date. Not so good if it's an old one from the early 1920s.

On 19 July 1940 Hitler issued his final appeal for a negotiated peace. It was rejected out of hand and as a result the Luftwaffe were at last given clearance to begin offensive operations against mainland Britain. Even so, they were ordered not to attack civilian targets. The first large-scale attack took place on 11 August when seventy-four bombers escorted by one hundred fighters raided Portland Naval Base. The attack should have been confined to purely military targets but due to a navigational error some bombs fell on populated areas resulting in the RAF mounting a retaliatory raid on Germany. Two weeks later a similar error saw bombs meant for London Docks fall on central London. Any other war leader might well have hung back but not Churchill. He ordered the RAF to take the battle to the heart of the Reich – to bomb Berlin itself. In doing so it brought about a dramatic escalation in the air war but at the same time diverted German resources and assets from their invasion build-up. Hitler was furious.

It was during December that Manchester would suffer two of its heaviest attacks. The raid came as no surprise as wireless traffic intercepts revealed that Luftflotte 3 units KG51, KG54, and KG55 had been assigned to attack the city and night fighter, anti-aircraft, and ARP services had been alerted. Within minutes of the city's sirens sounding on the evening of 22 December incendiaries were falling on and around Albert Square as the lead aircraft of Luftflotte 3 pathfinder unit KGr100 dropped its payload. Over the next thirty-eight minutes the eleven aircraft of KGr100 dropped nearly 10,000 incendiaries over the target area. Other early arrivals over the city included the first of five Heinkel IIIs of I/KG55 and the twelve Heinkel IIIs of II/KG55 which dropped a mixed bag of target illuminating flares, HE and incendiaries. What we have to remember is that all 149 aircraft taking part in the first phase of the attack weren't over at the same time - it took over three hours for the eighteen Ju 88s of KG77 to complete their business. It would be a drawn out affair lasting nearly five-and-a-half hours but as the minutes ticked by more and more aircraft arrived, many of them guided by the fires still raging around Liverpool and Merseyside which had been blitzed the previous night. The second phase, involving 121 aircraft of Luftflotte 2 commenced during the early hours of the morning some, forty minutes after the last of Luftflotte 3's bombers had turned for home.

Buildings in the Princess Street/Clarence Street area were soon alight and a shower of incendiaries was reported falling around Bridgewater Street. At the time the main threat for the MFB and AFS units was in the vicinity of Deansgate where the fire had taken hold of the Royal Exchange and the Victoria Building and the gas main outside Hailwood's Creamery in St Mary's Gate had been ruptured and was alight. Adding to Manchester's growing problems was the fact that a large number of pumps and their crews were still in Liverpool where they had been sent the previous night. It was Manchester's turn to call for reinforcements, some of which would come from as far away as Teesside. Before the raid was two hours old the Exchange Hotel was well and truly alight, Market Street was threatened and part of the Victoria Building had collapsed into Deansgate, blocking the thoroughfare from Blackfriars Street to Victoria Bridge. The road to Salford was severed when a building at the corner of Bridge Street and Gartside Street collapsed.

In the Portland Street, Sackville Street and Watson Street fires rampaged through a number of warehouses and a cluster of HE bombs ripped Gray Street, Stafford Street and Cooke Street apart. There were some lucky escapes. Around 450 people were trapped by debris in Gibson's shelter in Erskine Street but thankfully all were saved. In another incident a HE bomb scored a direct hit on a shelter in St George's Park. More by luck than judgement the shelter was empty at the time. In all, the dropping of 272 tonnes of HE and over 37,000 incendiaries had resulted in over 400 fires, of which at least a quarter were serious, and destruction on an unprecedented scale, the likes of which the city had never before experienced.

Fire and rescue crews were still at work the following evening when the alert sounded again – Luftflotte 3 was paying a return visit. The attack was led by ten Heinkel IIIs of Kgr100 which dropped over 9,000 incendiaries in a little over fifty minutes. The lead aircraft of KG1, 1/KG55, KG77 and 111/KG26 were over the city before 8.00pm, some of the crews aiming their payloads at fires they observed through gaps in the clouds. Others used their radio direction finding instruments, while some chose to make visual attacks. But it was the eighteen Heinkel IIIs of 1/KG28 that carried the surprise punch. Each was armed with two LM1000 parachute mines, the Luftwaffe's heaviest bombs, and aircrews reported seeing a number of huge explosions. By the time the all-clear sounded at 1.28am the city had been hit by at least fifty-five HE bombs with many others falling on Salford. Rescue Parties attended 501 logged incidents and pulled 226 people out of the rubble.

By about 3.00am on Christmas Eve morning the fires were contained even if many were burning furiously and additional fire fighting cover had arrived in the shape of a London Fire Brigade convoy of forty pumps and seven hose lorries. Then fate played a hand. A strong wind blew up carrying sparks and embers far and wide over the badly mauled Piccadilly area re-igniting some fires and starting fresh ones. Things got out of hand very quickly and a wall of fire extended from Moseley Street, across Piccadilly and beyond Portland Street, threateninged to penetrate as far as Princes Street. There was little alternative other than calling in the Royal Engineers to blast fire breaks.

The devastation within a square mile of Albert Square had to be seen to be believed. No less than 165 warehouses, 150 offices, five banks and 200 other business premises had either been destroyed or sufficiently damaged to make them unusable until repairs had been carried out. A further 300 warehouses, 220 offices, twenty banks, and 500 other business premises had been damaged to a lesser degree. Manchester's death toll over the two days stood at 376 with many hundreds injured. 30,000 houses had been damaged, many extensively, and 5,049 people made homeless by the raids were distributed around twenty-eight Rest Centres. By the beginning of January 1941 at least 13,000 houses had been patched up and only 1,600 people remained in Rest Centres, which during an eight-day period had looked after a total of 72,000 citizens.

The effects on Salford were heavy. An estimated 276 HE bombs, including parachute mines, and 10,000 incendiaries had rained down on the city, causing one conflagration, thirty-one major and about 400 large to medium fires. Local fire fighting cover had been overwhelmed and reinforcements from no less than fifty-nine outside brigades were called in. 8,000 houses and fifteen schools had been destroyed or damaged and 5,000 people made homeless. Casualties stood at 197 dead, 177 seriously and 648 slightly injured. Eighteen members of the police, fire and ARP services were among the dead and eighty-five had been injured.

At Stretford, 106 civilians had been killed, eighty-seven had been seriously injured and 184 were slightly injured. The housing stock had taken a hammering with no less than 12,000 affected resulting in 2,000 people made homeless.

Next to the two-night Blitz, the third heaviest raid began late on the night of 1 June 1941. It lasted just ninety minutes but was enough to see major fires and considerable damage done in the Derby Street, Oldham Street and Southall Street areas. Among the buildings damaged were the Assize Courts, the Gaiety Theatre, the YMCA, the College of Technology, and police headquarters in South Street. Salford was hit hard and among the casualties were fourteen nurses killed at the Salford Royal Infirmary.

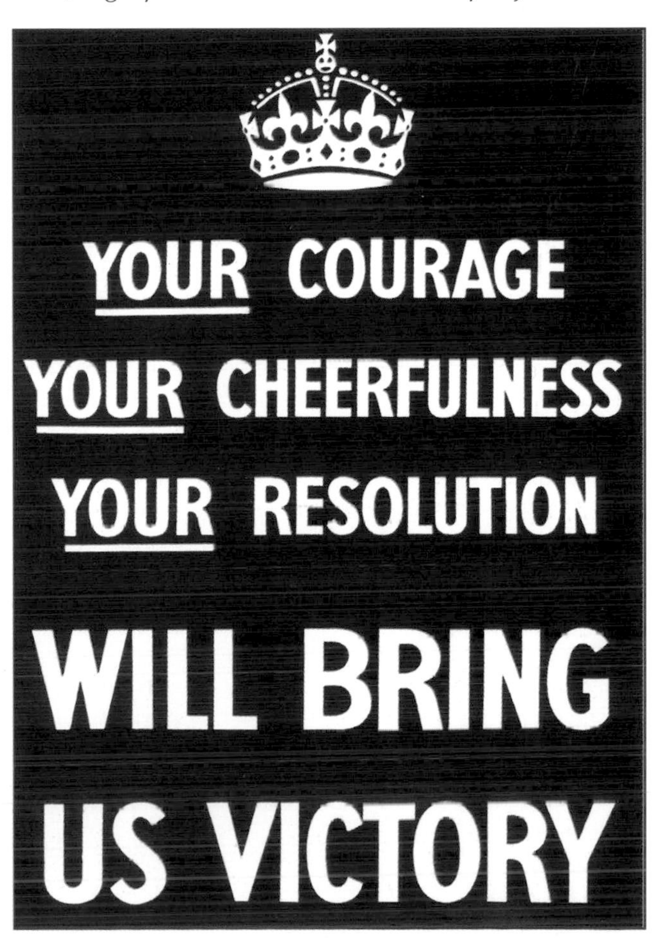

AIR RAIDS

SANIZAL DISINFECTANT

FOR

EMERGENCY SANITATION

SAN IZAL

DISINFECTANT

6D

Be prepared —

buy two bottles to-day

whilst you can still do so!

Newton, Chambers & Co. Ltd., Thorncliffe, nr. Sheffield

Almost every town and city has its 'famous' Blitz pictures. Perhaps the one image that has been acclaimed around the world is Herbert Mason's classic taken on 29 December 1940, of the unscathed dome and towers of St Paul's Cathedral rising majestically above a sea of smoke and flame. When it was published by the Daily Mail, it carried the caption 'War's Greatest Picture.' But the provinces also have their share of dramatic pictures. From Sheffield it is a row of burning: taken from the roof of the Sheffield Star by a photographer who was on fire watch. At Middlesbrough, Gazette chief photographer Teddy Baxter made his way through the falling bombs to photograph the scene of the destruction at the local railway station. He then rushed back to the office to process the images and get them off to London to the censors. Later that day he was hauled before the circulation manager and given a severe dressing down because he had punctured all four tyres on the van he had taken and the paper didn't know when it would be able to get replacements. At Hull one of the most poignant of pictures of its war is of the tower of the Prudential building – all that was left of a huge building that once stood at the junction of King Edward and Paragon Streets.

The series of pictures taken around Piccadilly at the height of the Christmas Blitz must surely rank among some of Manchester's most evocative images. This particular picture is looking across the gardens and bus station towards a major conflagration at the junction of Parker Street and Portland Street. It has to be remembered that when the bombs started falling Manchester's fire brigade was under strength as it had despatched thirty pumps and 200 men to help out at Liverpool. As the fires took hold the MFB were soon faced with taking some tough decisions. By the time the raid was over there were over 400 separate fires of which 100 were serious. Unable to fight them all simultaneously, the MFB had to decide which it would tackle and which it would have to leave to burn. In some instances the Luftwaffe made the decision for them as collapsing buildings and debris had blocked a number of roads making it impossible for fire engines, even manhandled trailer pumps to get through. In the foreground stands an AFS equipped saloon car complete with ladders and towing a trailer pump, waits to go into action. Its ghostly crew wasn't on the original picture; a Guardian artist added them for effect.

Only a few hours separates these two pictures of the warehouse fire at the junction of Parker Street and Portland Street.

This dramatic picture taken from Oldfield Road railway bridge, Salford, on Sunday 22 December, shows Manchester in flames. The tower of the Royal Exchange can be clearly seen, while over on the left the dome of the Ryland's building can be made out.

Tram wires are thrown about as they are hit by flying debris as Woolworth's store at the corner of Deansgate and St Mary's Gate collapses.

The crew and three passengers of this Salford Corporation bus must have felt pretty safe sheltering under Greengate railway arches. Unfortunately one of the bombs that fell on Exchange station plunged straight through into the arches and exploded killing all five on the bus.

The early hours of Monday 23 December 1940 found the fires at Exchange station burning out of control.

This picture was taken from the roof of the *Manchester Evening News* building at 8.00am on the morning of Monday 23 December. On the left is the Royal Exchange, second left, Victoria Buildings, front centre, Market Street and the Shambles, and in the distance at right is Exchange station. The picture was banned from publication until September 1941 and even then with a censored caption.

The bombed out remains of the Free Trade Hall after the Christmas Blitz. The destruction of the building left the Hallé Orchestra homeless. It also instigated a 30 year association between the orchestra and Belle Vue - as the Hallé found a new home in the Kings Hall. Sir John Barbirolli. the Hallé's legendary conductor praised the Kings Hall for its acoustics and atmosphere. Crowds of up to 6,000 sat enthralled as the Hallé performed.

Daylight found fire crews damping down a number of burned out warehouses – this particular building was on the corner of Portland Street and Sackville Street – our cameraman is looking towards Oxford Street. In the distance a blackout mask can be seen fitted to the left-hand tram wire. In order to minimise flashes from the trolley heads during air raids, drivers were instructed not to have the controller on power before they had engaged the trolley head to the wire. Drivers were also instructed to switch off power whenever the car was passing under breakers.

Damage at the corner of Miller Street and Rochdale Road. In the centre of the picture, to the left and slightly below the traffic light is a pre-war fire alarm. One of the numerous AFS crews sent to reinforce Manchester was that led by Stan Haggarth. Stan's AFS station was located at the Co-op bakery in South Terrace, South Bank, on the Tees. In the early hours of 23 December Stan and his crew were at Darlington where they met up with other AFS units from the north that were going to help out in Manchester and Liverpool. "We got more experience in a matter of days than you would get in months or years of peacetime firefighting," he commented. "Up to then I had never seen anything more than chimney fires and house fires – and I was suddenly pitched into a scene of six, ten and twelve-storey buildings well alight. On one occasion in Manchester we had to take over from a crew who had all been killed – with the remnants of their gear still lying around. We had to take over their equipment and carry on with the job they had been doing."

Fire crews snatch a wad and a brew from a mobile kitchen. The kitchen had been presented by the Order of the Eastern Star, Canada "to the people of Manchester."

Victoria station on the morning of Tuesday 24 December. The picture was banned from publication.

Many of the city's best known warehouses were reduced to smouldering wood, flame seared walls and mountains of rubble. This picture was taken from high on Lewis's building looking towards Portland Street.

This picture of smouldering ruins in the Cannon Street, Shambles, Market Place area, does not appear to have been submitted to the Press & Censorship Bureau until 1 December 1941. It was passed for publication two days later.

This picture, taken by a Guardian photographer on Tuesday 24 December, shows the damage to the Shambles, one of Manchester's oldest shopping centres. The picture was banned from publication.

Manchester Exchange before and after the debris had been cleared away.

An unexploded parachute mine at Watson Street railway yard off Deansgate. Among the aircraft of Luftflotte 3 that attacked Manchester on the night of 22/23 December, were eighteen Heinkel 111s of 1/KG28 (on temporary detachment from Luftflotte 2), each of which was armed with two LM1000 parachute mines. It was found that the 8ft 8inch long mine could be used against land targets when dropped by parachute – its skin was too thin to allow it to free fall. On release from the bomber, the rear cone housing the parachute was pulled clear by means of a wire attached to the fuselage of the aircraft, which in turn enabled the parachute to deploy. The weapon was fitted with a clockwork fuse, activated on impact, and timed to detonate twenty-five seconds after arming. Having a high, explosives to weight ratio, LM1000s caused considerable damage in built up areas. As can be seen, the tail cone on this particular mine is partially intact. Because parachute mines were primarily a naval weapon responsibility for defusing them was with the Royal Navy.

Several of the LM1000 parachute mines that failed to detonate fell amid houses, including one that crashed through the roof of 32 Dulcie Street, Chorlton-on-Medlock, to finish up embedded in the cellar. Others however did what they were intended to do. On 28 February 1998, the Evening News Family Memories' page carried Irene Pope's eyewitness account of a descending parachute mine. "We lived in Trafford Street, Salford, and our yard backed on to the yard of St Bartholomew's School, and we had brick air-raid shelters built round the outside toilets. My mother, gran, grandad and myself went into the shelter when the sirens sounded, but during a lull in the Blitz, the ladies went into the yard to enable grandad to use the toilet in privacy, when suddenly this mine came floating over the school yard. It was loosing height but we realised it was heading for the houses next to ours which had attics, so they were a storey higher than ours. Suddenly a gust of wind came. It seemed to twist the parachute and took the mine over our house, missing the next one literally by inches. But the tragic result was that it lost height when it reached Ordsall Lane and landed on an ARP post, killing all the wardens, who were colleagues of my father. He himself was an air-raid warden, but at the time was at another post."

And this is what happens when a parachute mine does what it is intended to do. This is Stretford High School after it had been ripped apart by a LM1000 mine dropped by I/KG28.

During a major raid, hundreds, sometimes thousands of properties would suffer light damage from numerous causes including flying debris, ground vibration and blast waves. What is left of the windows of this house had been covered over until such times as they can be properly replaced.

This is the damage caused when an incendiary crashed through the window of this house and set the furniture alight. Manufactured from a magnesium alloy, incendiaries were approximately thirteen inches in length and two inches in diameter, and when filled weighed two. A conical-steadying vane completed the weapon. They were usually packed thirty-six to a canister, which would burst open on release from the aircraft to scatter them over a wide area.

The Ministry of Information were always quick on the scene following major raids. One of their officers was Godfrey Baseley, the originator of BBC radio's The Archers. "I had to practically live in the van," said Godfrey. "Telling people how to obtain ration books, where to get clothing from, how to contact the council for repairs, where evacuation meeting points were and so on. I also relayed instructions from the Ministry of Food on such things as how to remove dust from butter."

The Press & Censorship Bureau, as it was deemed to show the fighting spirit, good humour and stubborn courage of your average Brit under fire passed this oft-reproduced image for immediate publication. This group of Manchester office workers have managed to salvage a few office documents but have been left with no office to work in.

Though the main casualties on the night of 9/10 January 1941 were at Whittington where nine people died when a surface shelter took a direct hit, a bundle of possessions heaped on a pavement in Gorton bears witness to damaged caused there. One of the dangers of piling stuff on the pavement like this was looting, a despicable act that had reached epidemic proportions: there were 4,584 cases in London alone during 1940. Looting, a capital offence under the Defence of the Realm Act, was widespread in such places as London, Liverpool, Manchester, Birmingham, Coventry, Sheffield and Glasgow. The Lord Mayor of London even called for notices to be posted that warned looters would face the death penalty. Many acts of looting were carried out by villains disguised as ARP, AFS, even military personnel, but just as many were committed by members of these organisations. In certain circumstances all of us would turn to looting food, medicines, fuel, weapons and ammunition if our very survival depended upon it. But to loot personal possessions from the dead, dying, and severely injured, or stripping homes of their entire contents save for the blackout curtains for nothing more than making a profit is something else. The law came down hard on anyone found guilty, though by today's standards many of the cases would only warrant a ticking off. There was the widow who was fined for 'looting' coal from the bombed-out house next door despite the fact that she'd been told it was okay to take the stuff. Then we have the case of the leader of a heavy rescue squad jailed for looting a near-empty bottle of gin from the ruins of a pub. The fact that he and his squad had risked their own lives searching through the pub's shattered remains for survivors was not taken into account. Having clawed their way through the wreckage he had noticed the bottle lying in the rubble picked it up and shared it with his men. That they most certainly deserved a drink was no defence.

On 11 March 1941, a three-hour raid resulted in damage across several districts including Stretford, Trafford Park and the Pomona Docks. During this raid the centre stand at Manchester United's ground took a direct hit, leaving the medical room destroyed and the changing rooms burnt out. This picture is of a bomb crater at the junction of Brunswick Street and Hyde Road. This was the first bomb in a stick of four.

The second bomb fell on the tiny Ardwick Picture House. The building to the rear of the damage is the Apollo Cinema.

A tangled mess of steelwork, ventilation trunking and timber occupy the area where the Ardwick Picture House screen ought to be.

The third bomb hit the artillery barracks

The fourth bomb damaged the Clarence Hotel, Hyde Road.

Neighbours in Seedley View Road, Salford, discuss damage to gardens and Anderson shelters, May 1941.

When the Guardian submitted this picture to the censor, it carried the following caption. 'The main railway line from Manchester to Derby blocked by sand and water after an air raid on morning 11 May 1941.' Initially, the Press & Censorship Bureau refused the paper permission to publish, but it appears the picture was resubmitted some time later. It was finally passed on 1 September but with the following censored caption. 'A railway line blocked by sand and water after a recent air raid.'

Salvage work underway at United's ground at Old Trafford. As well as virtually destroying the main stand and badly damaging the United Road Terracing, the heat generated by the ensuing fires badly scored the pitch. Club secretary Walter Crickmer, who ironically was to perish in the Munich Air Disaster of 1958, narrowly escaped death, having been buried in the rubble for several hours, suffering with arm and leg injuries and severe shock. For the remainder of the war United played their home games at Main Road. That didn't stop United thrashing City 7-1 on Easter Monday 1941. The 1941-42 season was probably United's best wartime season, as they came top of the Football League, Northern Section.

Rescue operations in progress in Meadow Street, Moss Side, May 1941.

This picture carries a date of 26 May 1941, but might be slightly earlier as the surviving copy in the Evening News archives does not carry a Press & Censorship Bureau stamp, though the caption has all the hallmarks of the censors. ' Men who volunteer their day off a week to help blitzed victims of a bombing.'

Taken in Deansgate on 2 June 1941, the morning after the city's third heaviest raid of the war. It will be some hours yet before these firefighters can call it a day.

The Assize Courts on the morning of 2 June. The picture was passed by the censor under the 28-day rule meaning that it couldn't be published until 30 June, and even then it had to carry a caption written by the censor which read: 'Extensive damage done by a bomb to a building in a North West town.'

The gaping hole torn in the nurses' home at Salford Royal Infirmary, where fourteen nurses were killed. On the right is St Phillip's Church, from which the Reverend James Hussey was walking to comfort the wounded at the hospital, when he too was killed by a bomb.

Demolition contractors Thomas Maiden Ltd were given the task of clearing the Victoria Buildings site. As with all photographs taken for publication, this picture was submitted for approval to the Press & Censorship Bureau. It was passed for publication on 6 August 1941, though the following caption had to be used. 'Good progress is being made with the clearing up of damage caused during the 1940 December 'blitz' on Manchester. Victoria Buildings in course of demolition.'

Taken in Piccadilly on 14 August 1941, this picture shows the progress made in clearing buildings destroyed in air raids. At the time there was a proposal to concrete over the vacant sites for use as a bus station.

Dating from September 1941, this picture shows the progress being made in clearing the damage in the Shambles.

On Christmas Eve 1941 an extraordinary raid took place that scared the living daylights out of thousands of Mancunians. At around 3.00pm, as hordes of people were out and about doing their last-minute Christmas shopping along Market Street, the unmistakable drone of bomber engines was heard overhead as three aircraft suddenly appeared with their bomb-doors opening menacingly. There had been no alert sounded, and the crowds, remembering the previous year's raid by the Luftwaffe, feared the worst. People scattered, bowling one-another over as they panicked. But the fear and panic soon turned to anger when they discovered what the bombers were dropping – ten thousand road safety leaflets from the Chief Constable of Manchester, John Maxwell. This wasn't the first leaflet raid over Manchester. On 8 August 1940, a German bomber dropped a bundle of leaflets. Unfortunately the bundle failed to open and plummeted to earth intact, landing upon the head of a police officer guarding the entrance to the Civil Defence Report and Control Centre, Salford.

HITTING BACK

A Royal Navy destroyer makes her way along the Manchester Ship Canal. On the night of 7/8 May 1941, the Luftwaffe concentrated its effort against the port installations of Liverpool, Birkenhead and Hull. However, a lone aircraft armed with two type B Luftmines was sortied to attack the Manchester Ship Canal tidal locks at Eastham. Thankfully the attack failed, for if it had been successful Manchester Docks (at sixty feet above sea level) would have been out of action for months.

HMS *Manchester* was one of eight warships belonging to the Southampton Class. *Manchester*, along with *Gloucester* and *Liverpool* formed the second group of the class. They were fitted with a second director control aft, had improved armour protection and carried more fuel. They carried the same armament as their earlier sisters: a main battery of twelve 6inch (Mk XIII) guns in four triple turrets; a secondary battery of four twin 4inch (Mk XVI) guns; a pair of quadruple 2pdr pom-pom anti-aircraft guns and four twin .5inch machineguns. They also carried two triple mount 21inch torpedo tubes and three aircraft.

In November 1940 HMS Manchester was assigned to Operation Collar, a fast convoy comprising ships for Malta and Alexandria. Sailing on 12 November, *Manchester* and her sister ship HMS *Southampton* acted as escort to the fast merchantman MV *New Zealand Star.* A separate convoy that included the liner *Franconia* and the Clan liners *Clan Forbes* and *Clan Fraser* were also put to sea. Several hundred miles off Gibraltar the *Franconia* and *Manchester* detached from the other ships to make a high-speed run to the island fortress where they were soon joined by HMS *Southampton*. At Gibraltar, the cruisers boarded over 1,300 RAF personnel from the liner before steaming out to rejoin the convoy.

As the convoy sailed east escorted by elements of Admiral James Somerville's Force H, units of the Mediterranean Fleet were heading west towards Sardinia. On 27 November, aircraft *Ark Royal* spotted an Italian force comprising two battleships, seven cruisers and a number of destroyers to the south of Sardinia on an interception course for the convoy. Force H and the Mediterranean Fleet's battleship HMS *Ramillies* turned to join battle. During the hour-long exchange of gunfire a general cruiser action developed. The heavy cruiser HMS *Berwick*, armed with eight 8inch guns engaged the *Pola* and *Fiume*. *Manchester, Sheffield* and *Newcastle* took on the *Trieste*, *Trento* and *Bolzano*. *Southampton* divided her fire between the *Fiume* and the *Gorizia*. During the action *Manchester* also badly damaged the destroyer *Lanciere*.

One of *Manchester's* quadruple 2pdr pom-pom AA mounts. During her refit in early 1941 her AA armament was beefed up with the addition of one 40mm Bofors and five single 20mm weapons.

A and B turrets of *Manchester's* main battery in action.

Taken during Operation Pedestal this picture shows *Manchester's* consort in the close-escort force, the cruiser HMS *Kenya* under attack. Both *Kenya* and her sister *Nigeria* were damaged.

Empty shell cases litter the deck around A turret.

On 2 October 1940, the Admiralty requested that a Guardian photographer be on hand at Barrow-in-Furness the following day. The Guardian wasn't told why the photographer was needed – that was still a secret - so our man was just as surprised as everyone else at the port when the Royal Navy turned up with a captured U-boat. The images, which were to be made available to all papers under the press rota agreement, were passed 'as censored' at 1325hrs on 4 October. The Press & Censorship Bureau insisted that the backgrounds be removed from the pictures prior to publication.

Just a few of the vast numbers of military vehicles landed at Manchester.

Manchester Division served throughout the war and was withdrawn in 1951.

After the Great War the Territorial Army was reorganised. The fourteen yeomanry regiments in the official table of precedence were to continue as horsed cavalry with the Lovat Scouts and Scottish Horse retained as scouts. Of the rest, twenty-five regiments converted to Royal Field Artillery (RFA), and eight regiments were reduced in strength to single squadrons but equipped with armoured cars. Of the remainder, the Montgomeryshire Yeomanry was absorbed into the Welch Fusiliers as an infantry battalion, and the reconstituted Middlesex Hussars converted to a signal regiment attached to the 2nd Cavalry Division. Two other regiments, the Lincolnshire Yeomanry and the exotically titled King Edward's Horse (The King's Overseas Dominions Regiment) were disbanded. Following Partition in 1922 the South Irish Horse were also disbanded. On the declaration of war in 1939, all fourteen senior regiments was still horsed, including both the Cheshire and the Duke of Lancaster's Own. In August 1940 the Duke of Lancaster's converted to artillery, forming the 77th and 78th Medium Regiments. The Cheshire Yeomanry was sent to the Middle East, where, as part of the 5th Cavalry Brigade, they continued to serve as mounted cavalry until March 1942. In June 1941, the Cheshires took part in one of the last mounted actions to be fought by the British Cavalry when they engaged Vichy French troops along the River Litani during the Syrian Campaign.

Traffic came to a stand-still on 29 September 1939 as the 8th (Ardwick) Battalion, Manchester Regiment marched through the city to entrain for France. At the time the battalion formed the 127th Infantry Brigade along with the 5th Manchesters and the 4th East Lancs and was part of the 42nd (East Lancashire) Infantry Division commanded by Major-General W G Holmes. The Division's home headquarters were in Manchester and other city-raised units serving with it included the 52nd (Manchester) Regiment Royal Artillery, and the 42nd Royal Tank Regiment. Manchester units were also serving with the 66th Infantry Division, including the 6th and 7th Manchesters, which with the 2nd/8th Lancashire Fusiliers comprised the 199th Infantry Brigade. Three locally-raised Royal Engineer units (255th and 256th Field, and the 258th Field Park Companies) were also assigned to the 66th. By the time the Germans launched their invasion of France, BEF strength stood at ten infantry divisions in three corps and a tank brigade supported by about 500 RAF aircraft of all types.

Squaddies do their daily physical jerks. When war was declared a number of Western Command's East Lancashire Area Territorial units not assigned to particular formations were in the Manchester area. They included the Duke of Lancaster's Own Yeomanry, the 1st and 2nd/9th Battalions Manchester Regiment, the 257th Field Company, RE and the 104th Supplementary Reserve Company as well as signals and other units.

It's foot inspection time for the poor bloody infantry.

Members of a mixed battery go to action stations. Female members operated the range finder and predictor while their male colleagues manned the guns.

Anti-aircraft battery range finder. Another important piece of kit was the predictor; electronically controlled and linked directly to the anti-aircraft gun. As its name suggests the predictor plotted the changing position of an aircraft and predicted the point at which the gun should be aimed.

Sound locators were an integral part of the early warning system for local anti aircraft defences.

Two different types of searchlights receive attention at a maintenance unit. The light on the left is from a fixed site and is mounted on small caterpillar tracks. The larger searchlight in the background is one of the Metrovick-built 150cm versions which were allocated to mobile batteries.

The Barnstormers concert party was raised from troops serving with North Midlands Ordnance. They were on tour in December 1944 with their pantomime Cinderella. Here Staff-Sergeant Hathaway (left) cuts a fine figure as one of the ugly sisters.

Troops stationed locally take time out to watch a concert party do its thing.

It was the stunning successes achieved by German parachute forces during the invasion of the Low Countries in May 1940 that convinced the Prime Minister that Britain needed similar troops. Within a few weeks the Central Landing School had opened at Ringway, the aim being to train a force of 5,000 parachute troops within two years. The CLS received its first intake in early July: 800 enthusiastic volunteers drawn from other units. Unfortunately the Army's target of turning out one hundred trained paratroops ever two weeks soon ran into trouble. Firstly, the RAF could spare just one Whitley II bomber (maximum lad ten men at a time). Secondly, there weren't any parachutes, with supplies only arriving several weeks later. Eventually, four Whitleys were made available and conversion to troop carrying mode was simple. They simply removed the rear gun turret and replaced it with a platform from which the trainees jumped wearing the standard rip-cord parachute as worn by RAF and Fleet Air Arm crews. Later the Whitleys were further modified. The ventral turret was removed thereby creating a hole in the floor through which the trainees could jump wearing static line chutes which automatically opened.

Because Ringway was often congested with new Fairey and Avro aircraft under test, all parachute descents were made at Tatton Park. By mid to late 1941 the parachute course had been finalised at two weeks, candidates having to complete eight successful jumps to qualify for the now famous red beret and parachute wings. Week one was devoted to various skills such as jump techniques and landing correctly - both of which were learned in a hanger. This was followed by learning how to exit from aircraft and balloons and culminated in a trip up in a Whitley so that the student could get a taste of what it was like to fly in a plane. Week two involved actual jumping. The first three descents -including one at night - were made from a balloon, followed by five from a Whitley.

This picture gives us some idea of the cramped conditions inside a Whitley. Normally the men would be split into two groups of five, one either side of the jump hole, but here they are playing sardines simply for the benefit of the camera. All trainees were volunteers. Many joined for the adventure; some out of curiosity, others simply for the extra pay. The failure rate was high – it still is today because the Parachute Regiment demands high standards. Those who either couldn't make the grade or decided, on reflection, that perhaps parachuting wasn't for them, were returned to their former units without repercussions.

An instructor goes through an equipment check with one of his trainees prior to making a jump. The static line chord that automatically opened the chute when the paratrooper exited the plane can be seen on the instructor's chute.

ATS girls get to learn a little about motorcycles courtesy of the Royal Artillery: Manchester Barracks, 7 September 1939. Many pictures taken during the early months of the war tend to depict ATS girls doing little more than office work or cooking for troops. This would soon change as the ATS took over other duties thereby freeing up their male colleagues for combat roles. Many ATS girls would be trained not only to take over driving duties on a wide variety of vehicles but also in motor vehicle maintenance.

ANNOUNCEMENT BY THE MINISTRY OF FUEL AND POWER

before you light a fire

(GAS · ELECTRIC OR COAL)

read this warning

Never since the war started has there been greater need for saving gas, electricity and coal than now. Before you switch on even another light pay attention to this. *Don't use more gas or electricity because you have less coal.*

INDUSTRY'S COAL SUPPLIES ALREADY CUT BY 10%

The need is so great that even industry's coal has been cut. Take that as a challenge and cut down the fuel you use — whether gas, electricity or coal. At work, help your fuel watchers in every possible way. At home, make use of coke you have in stock or any supplies you can get. Remember, every saving *you* make will be a direct aid to our Fighting Services, whose demands for coal are more urgent than ever and will not cease till Victory is won.

★ *A fire is easily lit with a sprinkling of small coal (½" to 2" in size) and the cinders from a previous fire. When it is going well, use coke alone. Go as easy as you can with gas and electricity — both coal in different forms.*

VITAL SAVINGS YOU SHOULD BE MAKING NOW

- Light a fire in one room only whether gas, electric or coal.
- Put fire bricks in your grate.
- Use your boiler only once a week.

EVERYONE must save more

FUEL for BATTLE

Home for Christmas. A Soldier and a member of the ATS walk down Hunts Bank at Victoria station.

During May 1941, Controller Knox, Inspector ATS, visited units in the Midlands and the north west.

For the ATS, office work and administration remained core roles. Our picture of recruits taking a typing lesson dates from 1942.

"Just sign here, here and here." As the women's services took on more and more responsibilities, numerous methods were used to attract recruits, including setting up recruiting booths in department stores.

ATS drivers collect their billeting allowance before starting out on a convoy of lorries. HRH the Princess Elizabeth trained with the ATS as a driver-mechanic. The story goes that the King visited her unit: who unbeknown to the princess, somehow got to her vehicle and removed the distributor. At the subsequent inspection the King stopped by his daughter's vehicle and asked her to start it up.

This picture is one of a sequence taken of a lorry convoy driven by ATS girls.

Unlike their British counterparts, Polish ATS girls received full weapons training.

Manchester Home Guard units parade in public for the first time on 28 July 1940, just five days after the organisation had changed its name from the Local Defence Volunteers. The units are relatively well equipped as supplies of battledress uniforms and army boots didn't become readily available until August. Trafford Park LDV was raised in May 1940 under the command of Lt Col Maxwell of Metrovicks. It started out at company strength and rapidly rose to battalion size.

Home Guard units line up for an inspection parade at Heaton Park. This particular company was raised from railway employees.

The Lord Bishop of Manchester conducts a drum head service at Manchester race course for the 43rd Lancs Home Guard on 11 August 1940.

A colliery Home Guard unit (some guards still wearing LDV armbands) get a demonstration on the use of Molotov cocktails.

Machine gunners of the 39th (Cheadle Hulme) Cheshire Battalion, Home Guard, at Gatley range.

By May 1941 Home Guard strength stood at 1,600,000 men, though more importantly it was now adequately armed with infantry weapons: rifles, grenades and machine guns. All training, particularly in weapons handling, was taken seriously, though the quality of training in infantry tactics often left much to be desired until the establishment of a number of street fighting schools, usually situated within cordoned off, bombed-out areas of major cities. After all, if the Germans did invade, many HG units would be fighting in built-up areas, street-to-street, house-to-house. In order to give the HG units as realistic training as possible, they were often pitted against regular troops.

Though taken on 12 May 1942, this picture of the latest addition to the Home Guard's arsenal – the Sten gun – wasn't passed for publication until the following August. A simple weapon: basically a tube and a spring, the Sten was cheap and quick to manufacture and gave the force a considerable boost in its automatic firepower.

This *Guardian* picture of a downed Ju 88 was passed for publication on 1 October 1940. Alas the original copy on the back of the image is missing, though it is believed that Czech airmen serving in the RAF shot down this aircraft.

The Lancaster Group of manufacturers comprised the Avro factories and Metrovicks in the Manchester area, Armstrong Whitworth at Bagington, Austin Motors at Longbridge, Vickers-Armstrong at Chester and Castle Bromwich, and the Victory Aircraft Corporation of Canada. Production reached its peak in August 1944 when the Group as a whole turned out 293 aircraft, with Avro accounting for 155 of them.

Our picture shows Leo Carter, a former bomber pilot serving with the Air Transport Auxiliary, a unit established in 1939 from volunteer men and women who held private pilot licences. The vast majority of ATA fliers' only experience was on light aircraft such as the Tiger Moth but they quickly found that their job entailed flying anything that needed ferrying between aircraft factories, RAF stations and maintenance units, wherever in fact the planes were needed. Many an ATA pilot would find themselves confronted with an aircraft they had never seen before. It might be the latest variant of a combat fighter or even a multi-engined bomber, with orders to fly it across the country without radio or navigation aids - just a book of instructions, an ordnance survey map or two, and equal portions of nerve and luck.

In December 1940 Ringway became home to a sub-section of Hawarden's Number 3 Ferry Pool, but the sheer volume of traffic saw the unit raised to a full ferry pool in its own right, becoming Number 14 FPP in July 1941. During the course of the war the pool's pilots would deliver over 6,000 Lancaster and Halifax bombers and hundreds of smaller aircraft to destinations all round the country. Most relied on 'Bradshaw' navigation - the art of following railway lines to lead them to their destination. Except for heavy bomber flights, ATA pilots flew alone and their greatest enemy wasn't the Luftwaffe but the weather. Once airborne the problem of getting below the cloud to navigate while avoiding the high ground of the Pennines or the Lake District was an ever-present danger. While based at Ringway, Leo flew 48 different types of aircraft including Spitfire and Hawker Tempest fighters, ground attack Hawker Typhoons, Dakota transport planes, Mosquito fighter-bombers, B25 Mitchells, Wellingtons and Hudsons. "We got our hands on anything that was going. We did not have any special instruction on these aircraft. I sometimes flew aircraft types that I had never seen before." The Ministry of Aircraft Production headed by Lord Beaverbrook employed ATA pilots. The idea of using civilian pilots came from Gerard d'Erlanger, a director of the pre-war British Airways. He wrote to the Air Minister, Harold Belfour, about it in 1938.

A barrage balloon in the process of being inflated. Manchester's balloon barrage was a part of No31 (Barrage Balloon) Group, which was raised on 1 April 1939 and had its headquarters in Birmingham. No10 Balloon Centre was located at Bowlee, Middleton, as was 926 (East Lancashire) Squadron, comprising three flights, each of eight balloons. The balloon defence of the city was in the hands of 925 (East Lancashire) Squadron, it too comprising of three flights each eight balloons. In 1940 the two squadrons were each equipped with forty balloons.

One of 925 (East Lancashire) Squadron's balloons at Swinton Fields in August 1940.

WOMEN WANTED

to take over the

BALLOON BARRAGE

The nightmare of Nazi airmen is Britain's balloon barrage. That's why it is one of the most important jobs in the country to keep those silver fish flying! And the WAAF have proved they can take over this important front-line job from the RAF!

It's a fine, healthy life for women who are fit and strong and fond of the open air. You must be 5′ 1″ or over, and aged between 17½ and 43. After a short training course, you will be posted to a balloon site. Sites are usually in or near a town. There you will live and work in a small community of about a dozen or so. When fully trained your minimum pay is 3/- a day *and all found.*

In addition to balloon operation, there are many other interesting trades open now in the WAAF. Every woman not doing vital work is asked to volunteer.

A Serviceman's wife does NOT lose her allowance on joining up, and she IS granted her leave to coincide with her husband's leave, subject only to urgent Service considerations.

Go to a Recruiting Centre* or Employment Exchange for fuller information. If you are in work, *they* will find out whether you can be spared from it. If you cannot go at once, send in the coupon.

When this girl joined the WAAF six months ago, to become a balloon operator, she was badly under weight. Now she's back to normal. "You can tell them from me, it's a grand life!" she says.

*Single girls born between January 1st, 1918, and June 30th, 1922, come under the National Service Act and *must* go to the Employment Exchange, *not* a Recruiting Centre.

297 Oxford Street, London, W.1 3010 *AR 10*

Please send me full information about the trade of Balloon Operator in the WAAF.

Mrs. / *Miss* ________ Cross out "Mrs." or "Miss"

Address ________

County ________ *Date of birth* ________ *In confidence*

WAAF

Because the manning of balloons twenty-four hours a day, frequently in bad weather, required physical strength, each balloon had a crew of two corporals and ten airmen. In the middle of January 1941, the Air Officer Commanding Balloon Command, was asked to consider a suggestion that the flying of balloons could be carried out by members of the Women's Auxiliary Air Force (WAAFs). Technical improvements to equipment, including the mechanisation of some of the handling, meant that great physical strength was no longer a prime consideration and had already enabled Balloon Command to reduce the number of airmen required for each balloon. On a cold morning in April 1941, twenty WAAF volunteers attended their first course at Cardington. By the end of June the WAAFs had more than proved their worth and before the year was out the RAF had transferred thousands of WAAF officers, NCOs and airwomen to Balloon Command. Balloon Command was open to healthy women over 5ft 1 inches tall and up to 43 years-of-age. The minimum rate of pay after training was 3/- a day, all found. Any married woman who enlisted and whose husband was in the services continued to receive her allowances and was to be granted leave to coincide with that of her husband, subject only to urgent Service considerations.

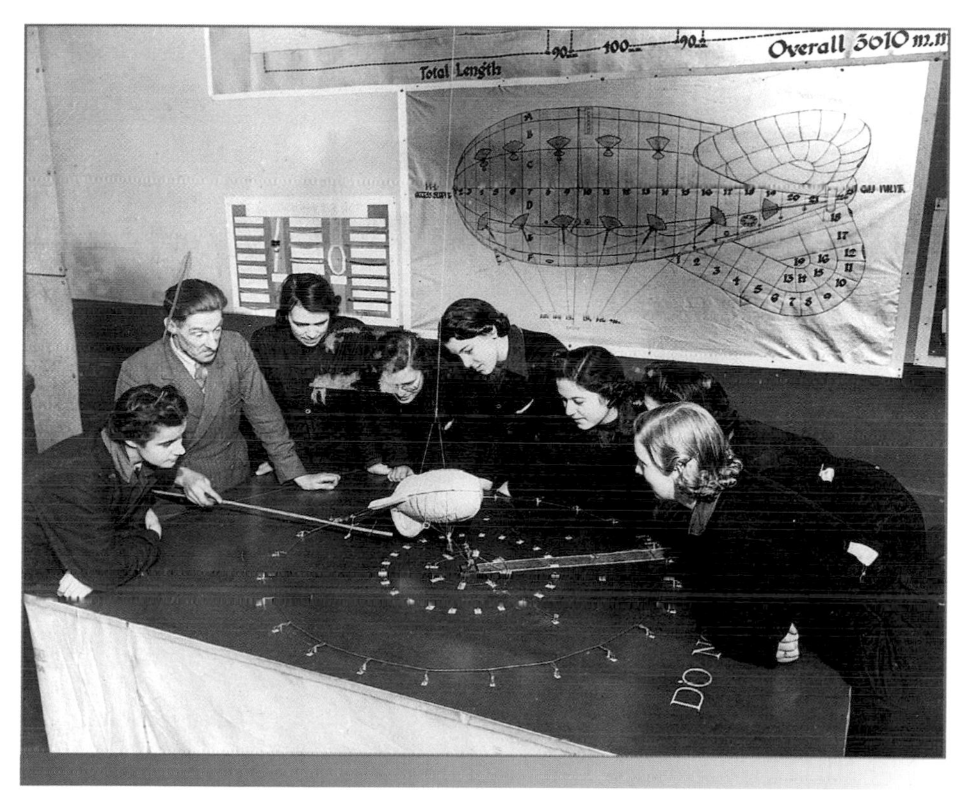

At first, the substitution of WAAFs for airmen on balloon sites wasn't as straightforward as it might appear. Even though technical improvements in balloon handling meant that physical strength was no longer a prime consideration, it still took sixteen WAAFs to replace ten airmen. Also, RAF balloon crews were integrated into military defence schemes whereas the WAAFs were non-combatants - unlike their Free Polish Air Force colleagues who received full weapons training.

THEY THINK IT'S ALL OVER

With the defeat of the Axis in 1945 most people expected life would return to pre-war conditions. Not so alas. The US government pulled the plug on Lend-Lease hurling the Labour Government into crisis. Britain was broke, the war had cost us £7.5 billion (about £320 billion at 2005 prices) and we lacked the US dollars needed to buy American goods. Our overseas debt stood at £3.3billion and export earnings only covered twenty-five per cent of imports. Austerity measures remained in force.

People were openly voicing opposition to the continuing measures. We had after all won the bloody war! Manchester Magistrates also caught the mood of the people. Two female Board of Trade inspectors had entered Sydney Goodman's shop intent on persuading him to break rationing regulations by selling them cloth without coupons: which he eventually did though he did charge them more than the regulation price. Magistrate Alderman Harry Lord asked the Board of Trade solicitor what would happen if a member of the public, had behaved in a manner similar to the two inspectors. "They would be prosecuted," replied the solicitor. "I thought so," said Lord, adding that inspectors had no right to be treated any different to ordinary members of the public then he threw the case out.

1945 was also the year that the City of Manchester Plan was published and those wanting to find out more about it should look at John J Parkinson-Bailey's excellent coverage in Manchester: An Architectural History. The plan was the work of city surveyor Roland Nicholas, city architect G Noel Hill, director of housing John Hughes, and Roy Hughes of the London, Midland & Scottish Railway. It was a radical rethink of the city centre: wide boulevards with wide pavements, car parking, the rezoning of industry, areas allocated for housing, retail and leisure, and a complete rethink on the road and rail layout.

The redevelopment of the city centre wasn't high on most people's list of priorities – what they wanted was a home. Nation wide only 200,000 new homes had been built during the war – a ninety per cent reduction on pre-war years. But now there were shortages of materials and skilled labour. After six years of war people's expectations were high. Surveys showed that the wartime philosophy of 'make-do and mend' had evaporated. People expected - no demanded - that new houses come with plumbed-in baths, inside toilets, hot running water and kitchens complete with the latest fixtures and fittings. The Housing Act of 1944 provided £150million to construct 250,000 homes on a temporary housing programme. The prefab was born. These bolt-together, single storey homes actually cost forty pounds each more than a traditional brick-built bungalow, but they came complete with fixtures and fittings far beyond those that most inner-city dwellers had been used to. Flush toilets, fitted kitchens, wash boilers providing constant hot water, and even a bit of a garden.

In June 1946 the government overreacted to a temporary fall in grain supplies by doing something that hadn't been done even in the darkest days of the Blitz – it imposed bread rationing. The announcement was greeted in the Commons with tense silence and Winston Churchill described it as "one of the gravest I have ever heard in peacetime." Food Minister John Strachey became the butt of numerous jokes, the Tories coining the slogan 'Starve with Strachey'. The adult ration was fixed at nine ounces a day, nearly a whole loaf, and there was an additional ration for male and female manual workers. By now the public's faith in the rationing system was totally undermined; they now grumbled when forced to queue up to an hour for a pound of sausages. The upshot would be the founding of the British Housewives' League by vicar's wife, Mrs Irene Lovelock. The League expressed the genuine feeling that people were sick to death of whinging politicians, austerity this, austerity that, and sick and tired of being ordered around.

On 28 August 1947 newspapers reported that, 'Britain last night went back to a war footing with the announcement from 10 Downing Street of the Government's super-austerity plan. Main points in the plan are that foreign holiday travel will be banned after October 1st; basic petrol ration will be abolished from the same date; and the meat ration reduced from 1/2d to a shilling from September 7th.
It is not expected that more than 2d worth of meat will be canned meat, and at times the ration will be all carcass meat. The tea ration remains at the present two ounces. Ration books must be surrendered after two nights in a hotel, whereas previously the limit was four nights; and restaurant and hotels will have a cut from fifteen to eighteen per cent in food supplies from next Monday. Canteens are not affected, nor are places not charging more than 2/3d a head for any meal.' However there had been some let-up in rationing for expectant mums. They were allowed an extra pint of milk a day, extra eggs and an extra half ration of meat. They were also entitled to receive vitamins and concentrated orange juice and had priority for bananas and oranges as and when shipments arrived.

There was always plenty of advice in March 1949 on how to stretch the meat ration. 'When there are only a few small pieces of meat left over, the housewife is often puzzled how to turn them into an attractive dish that will serve another meal. Mash some boiled or steamed potatoes while they are still warm, adding salt and pepper and a little hot milk or melted margarine. Chop up some left over corned beef into tiny pieces, and mix them with the potatoes, adding a very little amount of horseradish sauce.

Melt some fat in a frying pan, make the meat and potato mixture into a large pancake, and fry brown. If preferred, the mixture can be baked in a pie-dish in the oven – in this case less fat is needed.' Yummy!

VICTORY SPECIAL

Manchester Evening News

END OF WAR IN EUROPE

Enemy Foreign Minister's Announcement

DOENITZ ORDER: "ALL GERMANS SURRENDER"

Doenitz Calls Off the U-boats

"GOEBBELS' BODY FOUND IN BERLIN"

"No Escape for War Criminals"

British Push South From Rangoon

Frames for First Six New Houses

Balcony Hope

"Lord Haw-Haw" Nal in Dublin

No News Of King Leopold

Germans Told "No Beer"

TATTOO

THE POLICE STAND BY—JUST IN CASE

And the reason for the advice was that Dr Edith Summerskill had just announced in the Commons that the meat ration was to be cut to 8d of carcass meat a week. Not only were housewives wondering how on earth they were gong to put decent meals on the table, butchers were scratching their heads over how they were going to cut carcasses into eight-penny portions. A trainee journalist was despatched around the city to see what local butchers thought. One said, "In future customers will be asked to bring their ration books every time they collect their meat, to make sure of their supplies. It is certainly going to be a job to make the meat go round, having to cut it into such small pieces. When customers realise just how small the ration is, I think they will wait until the weekend for their joints. I cannot see any advantage in having meat two or three times a week when it is so meagre. Some people have already decided to have a double ration next week, which means making up their meat once a fortnight."

Towards the end of the decade the country's financial position eased thanks to the Labour Government's efficient handling of the economy while their decision to devalue the pound in 1949 helped boost exports.

There was dancing in the streets as news of Germany's surrender spread throughout Manchester. These revellers were in Piccadilly Gardens. At Trafford Park there were scenes of confusion as hundreds of workers turned up to clock-on only to be told to go home. Many were under the impression that the VE-Day national holiday did not begin until after Churchill's scheduled 3.00pm official radio broadcast. By 10.00am however several hundred people had gathered in Albert Square to watch the raising of the flags of the forty-four allied nations. They were to be disappointed as a town hall official declared that the ceremony could not possibly take place until after the broadcast.

Revellers in the city centre during the early hours of VE-Day. Though the war was officially over, fighting continued in Czechoslovakia until 13 May and two days longer than that in Yugoslavia as Tito made an unsuccessful attempt to grab a chunk of Italy. Tito was thwarted by C Squadron 1st Derbyshire Yeomanry and a battalion of the Rifle Brigade, who were ordered to take up positions along the line of a river to the east of Udine. While there, word came through that a fully equipped German army corps of 90,000 troops was making a fighting withdrawal towards the Italian border. Yeomanry officers met with the German commander who made it quite plain that though he was more than willing to surrender to the British he would not turn his men over to the tender mercies of Tito's Partisans. The following morning Tito deployed his armour to trap the Germans on the left bank of the River Drau. The Germans depressed their 88mm flak guns and used them against the tanks with devastating effect. Once over the river the Germans surrendered. Tito's victorious Partisans executed around 30,000 Germans, Chetniks and fellow Yugoslavs who had chosen the wrong side. The Western Allies went on to betray the surrendered White Russian and Cossack forces who had fought for Germany against the USSR. Despite assurances that they could settle in the West, they were in fact handed over to the Soviets and thousands were summarily executed. Estimates vary as to the number of people who died within two years of the war ending from war-related problems. It ranges from two to five million.

The residents of Rumford Place, Chorlton-cum-Medlock, turn out for the Evening News photographer on VE-Day. The large Union flag is painted on the side of their communal surface shelter.

VE celebrations at Crumpsall Lane School. These children would be among those who would benefit from the Education Act of 1944. It abolished fee-paying in secondary schools enabling many more children to stay on beyond the minimum leaving age. Sixth forms in grammar schools became much larger than they had ever been.

LAST EDITION EXTRA

Manchester Evening News

FRIDAY, AUGUST 10, 1945

LEWIS'S

THE JAPANESE SURRENDER

One Condition—That Emperor Remains

"WE ACCEPT THE POTSDAM ULTIMATUM," SAYS TOKYO

JAPAN surrendered to the Allies to-day on one condition. She accepted the Potsdam Ultimatum, stipulating only that the Emperor's position as Sovereign Ruler should be safeguarded.

At 12 42 this afternoon a dramatic flash announced that the Tokyo Government had asked the Swiss and Swedish Governments to transmit a communication to Britain, the U.S.A., Russia, and China.

Immediately afterwards Tokyo Radio announced the Japanese decision in the following terms:

"GOD-SENT RULER"

Flash That Told "The End"

How Japan Gave News

Crowds in City Cheer the End

The World is at Peace

The Russian Advance

8,000 Will be Freed

"Read all about it! Japs surrender." The Japanese fought fanatically for every inch of territory and it seemed that the war in the Far East would drag on well into 1946. It was estimated that a direct assault on the Japanese home islands would cost the allies 800,000 casualties. On 6 August 1945 an atomic bomb was detonated over the city of Hiroshima. Three days later Nagasaki suffered a similar fate. On 14 August the Japanese government accepted unconditional surrender and the formal capitulation was signed on board the US battleship Missouri.

VJ-Day party in Richmond Street, Moss Side.

VJ-Day street party at Heaton Park.

You can't help feeling that many of these ladies at the Ferranti Works at Moston just want to leap around and cheer their heads off. Perhaps they did just that after these pictures for posterity were safely in the can.

The demolition men attract a small but interested crowd of onlookers as they set about ridding Hulme's streets of their surface shelters.

On a rain-swept, breezy day in August holidaymakers watch Blackpool's victory tram as it trundles along the prom.

Winston Churchill resigned as Prime Minister on 23 May 1945, forming a caretaker government until Parliament was dissolved on 15 June. Churchill dominated the Conservative campaign, proving himself an excellent wartime leader: refusing to quit London at the height of the Blitz, and never afraid to openly show his emotions at people's suffering. However he proved something of a liability when, during his first election broadcast, he claimed that if Labour got into power they might form a British equivalent of the Gestapo. Labour won with a majority of 183 and Clement Atlee became the new Prime Minister. Churchill went to Buckingham Palace in a chauffeur-driven Rolls-Royce; Atlee turned up in a Standard Ten driven by his wife. Within three years of taking office, Labour had nationalised the railways, coal mines, utilities, airlines, and other key industries. The NHS came into being on 5 July 1948 with Minister of Health Aneurin Bevan stating that in its first full year the service would cost £249 million. Within twelve months the NHS had issued over 200million free prescriptions, 4.5 million pairs of spectacles, and 8.5 million people had been able to take advantage of free dental care. A concession was made to consultants in that they could treat their fee-paying patients in NHS hospitals rather than at private consulting rooms.

'Suit you sir!' Lt Leonard Roberts was the 250,000th customer at the civilian clothing depot in Oldham. The clothing ration in 1945 was forty-eight coupons. A man's suit made from utility cloth took twenty-four coupons, and servicemen being released from the forces could make a small fortune selling their demob outfits. In Civvy Street the suit would cost £12, the shirt 25/- and then there were two collars, two pairs of socks, a tie, a raincoat, a felt hat and a pair of shoes. The Army valued the lot at just £11 but on the black market the price could be upped as the buyer stood to save at least fifty-six coupons.

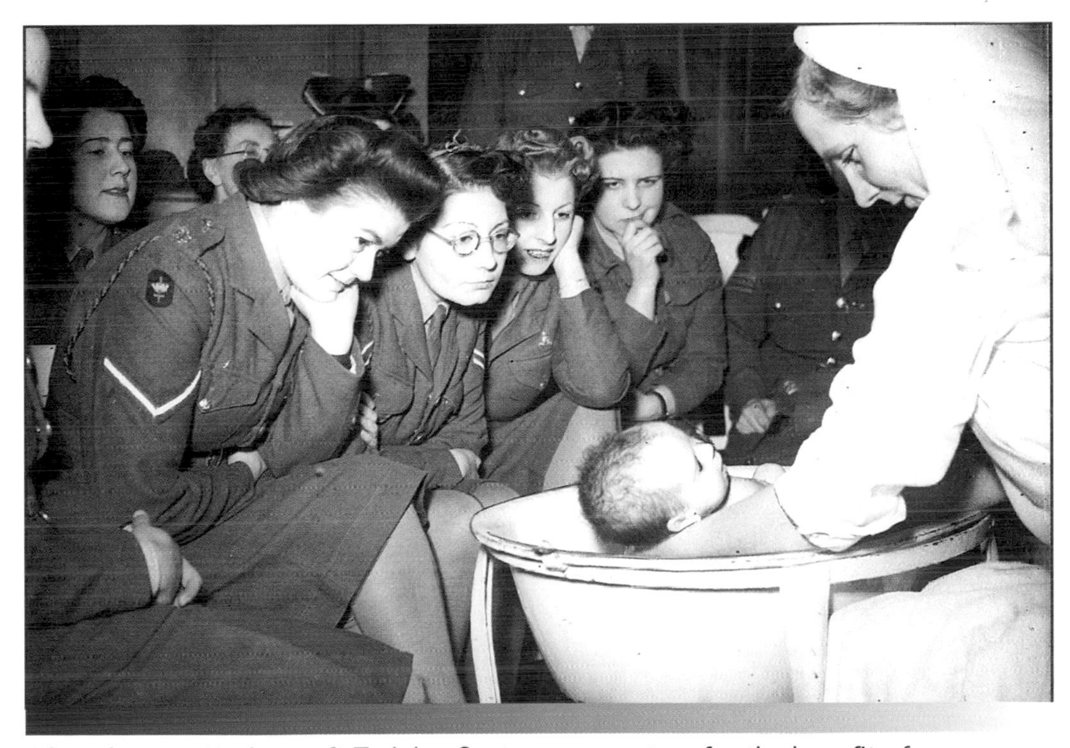

After the war, Mothercraft Training Centres were set up for the benefit of servicewomen who were shortly to return to civilian life. This particular baby-bathing parade was held for ATS girls on 5 December 1945.

One of the immediate post-war crises faced by Britain was a chronic housing shortage. Only 200,000 new houses had been built during the war while over 700,000 properties were still awaiting repair or demolition following war damage. It wasn't unknown for desperate families to take over abandoned military installations. These Nissen huts at Birch Hall Lane were given over to civilian occupation. Rents ranged from 8/3d to 11/3d a week. There was only one water tap and no sanitation.

The Bank of England building, Kings Street, February 1946.

A 1948 view of Ardwick Green.

'You wait hours for a bus then three turn up together!' One alleged benefit of the abandonment of the tram system was that it made road improvements easier. But at Ardwick Green where trams had once trundled through with relative ease, 'progress' had dictated the construction of this hastily conceived traffic island from the Liquorice Allsorts school of traffic management. 1 July 1949.

Albert Square was afflicted with the same disease as Ardwick Green. Newly installed curbing at the junction with John Dalton Street and Cross Street.

The Free Trade Hall in 1949 looking vastly different from earlier Blitz images.

One of Manchester's lost buildings – the Hippodrome – was still in full swing in November 1949 with the twice nightly variety show *Would You Believe It of 1949*, starring Pete Collin.

Rush hour commuters in 1946 could buy their tickets before boarding their buses or trams. Here conductor Edward Wilding is on duty at Piccadilly bus station punching a few of the 1,500 or so tickets he issued every evening.

By New Year 1949 only one tram route remained (No35 Exchange – Hazel Grove); a joint service operated in conjunction with Stockport, for which Manchester retained thirty-five cars – the last survivors of a fleet that had once been nearly 1,000 strong. The service converted to motorbuses on 9 January, and Manchester employed its last trams the following morning when five cars were used during the morning rush hour. Afterwards, four cars took part in closing procession, with No1007 bringing up the rear as the official last tram. The last tram carried the Lord Mayor, Alderman Mary Kingsmill Jones and other civic dignitaries.

All thirty-five withdrawn trams were taken to the Hyde Road depot, where, on 16 March, they were destroyed in a controlled fire by the MFB. The final act in the destruction came on the 4 May when the tramways' remaining four works cars were put to the torch.

Manchester Dry Docks had plenty of work on when this picture was taken in March 1946.

Manchester honours its local regiment for a job well done. The Freedom of the City of Manchester – the right to march through the city with drums beating, colours flying and bayonets fixed – was granted on 31 July 1946, the official ceremony taking place on 19 October.

Queen Elizabeth pays a visit to the Manchester Regiment at Dunham Park, Altrincham, in June 1948. She is seen here inspecting the Colour Party.

On 16 June 1946 a crowd of onlookers gather to watch the departure of the first scheduled civilian flight out of Ringway: an Air France Dakota bound for Paris. The total number of passengers flying out of UK airports during 1938 had been 70,000. During 1948 that figure increased to 914,000.

This is Ringway in April 1948 when crowds from far and wide flocked to the airfield for the first full-scale air show since before the war. Organised by 613 (City of Manchester) Squadron, Royal Auxiliary Air Force, the star of the show was the *Nene Lancastrian* (the large aircraft in the centre foreground). The plane was a civilian development of the Lancaster heavy bomber though this one differed from its sisters in that its two outer Merlin engines had been replaced with Rolls-Royce Nene turbojets thereby allowing it to stake a claim to being the world's first jet liner. Over to the right are the eight Spitfires of 613 Squadron and an Avro Anson. The fighter to rear left of the *Lancastrian* is a Rolls-Royce Griffon-engined Fairey Firefly trainer. The Firefly was a two-seat reconnaissance plane of which 1,623 were built during the war by Fairey's plant at Heaton Chapel and Hayes and also by the General Aircraft Co. Production continued after the war and the Firefly saw combat in the Korean War. The last Firefly was delivered in 1956.

A later variant Spitfire at Ringway. The Griffon-engined Mark21, 22 and 23 Spitfires entered squadron service too late to take part in the fighting. This particular machine was also photographed at Squires Gate, Blackpool, in July 1947.